CW00522382

RECLAIM YOUR POWER

ESCAPE THE CHAOS ON A 90-DAY JOURNEY

STÉPHANIE ESCORIAL

RECLAIM YOUR POWER: Escape The Chaos On A 90-Day Journey by Stéphanie Escorial - Akashabe Ltd.

Copyright © 2021 by Stéphanie Escorial

Copyright © 2021 by Akashabe

All rights reserved. No Portion of this book may be reproduced in any form without permission from the author. For permissions contact stephanie@akashabe.com

Permission to use material from other works: Dr. Bruce Lipton, Alice Bracegirdle, C. Wilson Meloncelli, James Clear, and from the Public Domain.

ISBN: 9798732128413

DISCLAIMER

The content of the book is for informational purposes only and should not be construed as any health-related advice. The information in this book is not intended to diagnose, cure, or treat any disease, illness, medical condition or mental disorders. If you have an existing medical condition, mental disorder or injury, make sure your doctor (physician or GP) or mental health care provider approves of any practice in this book. Your health is your responsibility. Use of this information implies your acceptance of this disclaimer. Any information you decide to use is done at your own risk.

Readers should know the websites listed in this book may change.

AKASHABE LTD
71-75 Shelton Street
London
WC2H 9JQ
United Kingdom

CONTENTS

This book is dedicated to Mum and Dad,
the Divine and all my Loved Ones.

ACKNOWLEDGMENTS

This book is a collective result of all my teachers, coaches, and various life experiences. Thank you.
I am grateful for all paths I have crossed, and for every person who consciously and unconsciously impacted my life.

I humbly thank the Divine Consciousness for always supporting me in my Mission.

I thank my lineage of Powerful Women, my Ancestors who have brought me here, my Beloved Family, who I cherish with all my heart, and my Friends who keep my feet on the ground.

Thank you to the Inspirational Teachers who have given me permission to use the material and quotations from their work.

Much love to you all,
Stéphanie Escorial

INTRODUCTION

Life becomes a struggle when we give our power away.
Many of us allow our outer world to dictate our inner world; thus, we give our power away and lose control.
Being in your power is all about reclaiming what we once lost.
It is retrieving yourself, if you like, the 'conscious, empowered being.'
We have been so conditioned growing up, projected by perceived authorities, parents, caregivers, society, and I could go on, about how we should live our lives, that we have forgotten who we really are. Thus we are not really living our own lives. You may think you have liberty and freedom, but if you really ponder this, do you?

Do you have self-control, self-trust? Do you work in the profession you have always imagined? What did you want to do as a child? Did you have any dreams and did you follow them through?

Empowerment is not about power poses; faking it until you make it, or being a bulletproof individual.
It is about being the raw, authentic you—and who are you really?

Reclaim the person you once were; reclaim your life.

If you think about it, not reclaiming your power, your life, yourself would be like living a half-life, really. You may look back and feel dissatisfied, or perhaps you will reflect on why you did not have the courage to live the life that you truly wanted. It is ok if you feel that way. Most of us conform to life that is comfortable and secured. I know I have.

You can choose differently at this moment.

If you are here reading this book, you are probably fed up with the struggles in life and feeling powerless, not in control of your life, and most likely unaware of how to change it or turn it around. I am sure you are feeling drained, perhaps stressed out or living anxiously, and you have probably tried a few courses or workshops, or read books that have not really helped you.

So you are probably wondering what is different about this book.

Well, for one, I have been in your shoes, and I believe all my hellish experiences happened for a reason: my Mission to help you take back your power, thus reclaiming who you truly are.

Before, I felt utterly powerless, not in control of my life. I kept giving my power away, not trusting or believing in myself, and that was all ok for a while. However, there came a time when I really needed to address the issues and rise above them by addressing my inner world.

I am offering you an inside-out experience, and some of you may be asking exactly what that is.

An inside-out experience is tending to your inner world in order to shift your outer world.
Your life is a mirror of your inner world. Some of you may protest, but if you really take the time and reflect on this for a moment, you may find your deepest fear—perhaps a fear you have been avoiding, suppressing or numbing—which really is ultimately the gateway to your power. Have some themes or patterns repeated themselves in your life? Perhaps a love or work situation repeats the same old issues dressed in different people or jobs?

Right here are your clues.

If you are reading this book, call me crazy, but your soul, your higher self, guided you here. There are no coincidences in life. All are perfectly designed. You may have come here because you are fed up with your struggles; you are fed up with being in similar relationships that deplete you. Perhaps you are so worn out that you have no zest in life, and you are unsure why.

Whatever the reasons, I want to help you RECLAIM YOUR POWER, and with that, you will RECLAIM YOUR LIFE and RECLAIM YOURSELF.

You have lost yourself along the way, which is more than ok. I have been there, at a point where I felt exhausted and thought to myself, *What is the point of all this?* This led me into depression. I did not know where I was going in life; I had lost a spark within myself, and again I felt that way after a terrible relationship. For me, relationships are great for seeing the wounds. They all reveal very uncomfortable traumas, but those are the gateways to your growth, the key to your wisdom.

One relationship led me to my awakening, set me on a self-discovery path. I turned all that pain into my purpose, and now I am here for you, to help you and guide you in taking back your power. I am here to give you a bit of a shake-up, if you will, to do the work. This book is for committed individuals who genuinely want change in their lives.

I will help you do so by giving you a 90-day plan. Why 90 days, you may ask?

Most clients I coach are for 90 days or 180 days, and they have experienced significant changes throughout those periods; however for you, it may differ, but the 90-day plan will give you a push to get you in the habit of doing the inner work, and align you with your higher self.

The Personal Power Life Method

The Personal Power Life Method is a 90-day plan, which covers self-reflection questions to reveal beliefs that are not supporting you, journal prompts, meeting your needs, re-parenting the inner child, grounding, fragmentation clearing, self-care, the nervous system, the neutral observer, and most important of all, the four components which I developed throughout this work, which I believe you will gain during this journey:

Awareness (Self-Awareness)
Clarity
Empowerment
Growth (Evolution)

Are you ready to do the work to reclaim your power?

GET YOUR FREE KIT

Get Your **Free Power Starter Kit** which will support you throughout this journey.
Visit https://stephaniescorial.com

The Free Power Starter Kit includes:

1. The Balancing Breathing Guided Audio to balance your energy and steady your nerves any time.

2. The Deep-rest Breathing Guide Audio to crush stress and anxiety, and to improve sleep.

3. A 90-day Calendar.

4. A 90-day Journal.

5. The Higher Power Weekly Ritual.

6. The Inner Child Journal.

If this book helps you in any way, I would appreciate it if you could take a few minutes to leave me a review. This will help and allow other readers to decide whether it is a suitable match for them.

My Mission is to *empower people* with simple, effective tools to Unleash their Full Potential in Life. If you wish to take part in this Mission, please point them to this book or the services we provide.

Thank you,
Stéphanie

TESTIMONIALS

Stephanie has been absolutely phenomenal as a life coach. She gives a you a safe space to talk and share your thoughts. More importantly, she guides you with tailor-made, effective tools to handle situations that have proven difficult. She gets you to change your thinking habits and any limitations you may have placed upon yourself.
Her approach is holistic and healing and she encourages you every step of the way with diligence, compassion, patience and sage words.
As a result of this, I came away a lot more self aware, at peace, knowing I have tools that can help me in my journey.
I would highly recommend her as a life coach.
- Kat, Designer.

Stephanie's breathing techniques have been really beneficial. It allows you to take time out and be present with various breathing techniques, which you are eased into. Stephanie structures the sessions well and informs you about the effect of the different techniques. I especially loved hearing about the science behind it.
You never flounder beyond the sessions because they are supported by easy-to-follow sound recordings that help you remember them.
I can honestly say that the breathing techniques can take the edge off in stressful moments, help you prepare for an activity, relax in general or just before you sleep (that one is my favorite!)
I would highly recommend Stephanie as a Breathing Coach.
- Kat, Designer.

"Steph is not so much a coach as a mentor - instead of telling one what to do, she provides a sounding board that enables one to develop one's own tools to deal with various problems that might occur in life. With patience and forbearance she provides a non-judgemental environment within which to explore issues that are of concern to the client and then works through a series of though exercises that are both apposite and effective in dealing with the issues under discussion. Having been under her mentorship for 5 weeks, I have been able to become more focused and positive in my own life and I feel that the positivity that I have learnt to discover in myself will continue well beyond the end of the mentoring period."

- Andrew. C

"To pierce through the illusion of separateness, to realize that which lies beyond duality — that is a goal worthy of a lifetime.
Simplicity is the ultimate sophistication."
Leonardo da Vinci.

STAGE 1

ESCAPE THE CHAOS

IT'S NOT YOUR FAULT

It wasn't my fault I grew up a shy child; I hid and stayed out of his sight. I would wrap myself around Mum's skirt when he was around, peeking out for 'possible threats.' Mum became my comfort zone, a haven providing me with unconditional love.

Dad's conditional love was somewhat distorted and hurtful. I did not feel safe around him, wounded by his pain, projected onto me. The wounds were never mine to begin with, but how could I have known this? It was in my later years that I finally learned to accept them and take responsibility.
Dad was my first distorted masculine energy, exposing me to a 'distorted truth.' I wanted his love as any other child would, but it was hurtful, and I felt rejected. All I knew from the distorted masculine energy was a tremendous amount of pain, so I hid from him. If he did not see me, he could not hurt me.

Over the years, I sought romantic relationships to heal the wounds I felt from my father. I was not conscious or self-aware, and I knew nothing about the dynamics of relationships. Unknowingly we seek romantic relationships to heal the wounds our fathers and mothers, the first prominent models in our lives, have projected upon us. If it is not parents, then it is grandparents or caregivers modeling those two energies. Do not get caught up on the mainstream definitions out there. I refer to the Masculine and Feminine as energies

1

derived from Creation - Masculine being Consciousness and Thought Form and the Feminine being Sound Field and Essence. One cannot live without the other.

In Hinduism, the two cosmic energies are Shakti and Shiva, from Creation, the Divine Consciousness. We are all made from these cosmic energies, Masculine and Feminine energies, regardless of gender. Our purpose is to transcend both and be one with Creation, All in one, Divine Consciousness, or Divine Whole.

Shiva is Consciousness, Thought Form, Paternal Love, the Masculine principle.

Shakti is Power, Energy, Maternal Love, the Feminine principle.

Most romantic relationships are transactions. I am sure some of you may protest, and it may not apply to you. However, some romantic relationships may look like this: Offer me love, and I will provide it back; do not hurt my ego, and I will not hurt yours until the honeymoon period phases out. Then the bubble bursts, and suddenly they cannot stand each other. The wounds come up, and the fights begin, not realizing that the mother and father wounds are at play. The unconscious partners blame each other for their unresolved pain. However, they are all opportunities to heal (heal and health derive from the Old English word haelen, meaning 'whole') and notice the wounds being presented in order to transmute them.

It is relatively uncommon in our modern society for us to be taught the importance of resolving our wounds or emotional mastery, so we numb them and ultimately grow beliefs that do not serve us, creating limitations in life. Eventually, the beliefs fester into the subconscious mind, creating a 'false ego persona.' None of us is exempt from this. We live in a collective traumatized world, and it is up to us to be accountable and take back control of our lives.

It is not a simple task; we have built a false ego persona over the years, a character based on limiting beliefs, programming stemming from society, culture, parents, caregivers, teachers and so on, mostly coming from the external world and mostly having nothing to do with you and who you are. Are you really living your own life? Is it based on people's views, parents, society, or culture? Or are you really living your truth? A life you truly want? I invite you to ponder on this. On the surface level, you may say yes, but if you dig deeper, you may find something you have been putting off your entire life.

It is not a straightforward task unlearning all that you have learned all those decades; it is leaning towards an 'ego death,' and that is not to be taken lightly. Do not let it put you off from doing the inner work, but I prefer to prepare you first before diving into this journey. I have been there, defending the self-image, and my false ego persona meant more than remembering who I truly am.
Doing the inner work may seem like a lot of effort, but the path of the false ego persona is far more exhausting and repetitive and keeps you in a loop with no way out. Your false ego persona is going to resist, with distractions or excuses such as 'I do not have the time,' 'what is the point,' or perhaps 'this is all nonsense.' It will come up with justified reasons to prevent you from doing the inner work, but if you are reading this book, perhaps it is time to wake up to your true self, your higher self.
The way to combat resistance is through action; it is an opposing force, a natural law. Every time you move up a level, resistance will equally oppose the 'expansion of self.' For every three steps you take in order to expand your consciousness, the opposing force will take three steps to hold you down.

As I did my inner work, resistance would show up as busyness for me. I was too busy in life to invest time in myself; I thought to myself, *It can wait; I have other important things to do*, or *I am fine as I am; I do not need this*, but as life reflected more distortion, I had to take action.

Resistance can also show up through distractions, tending to your housework when you can do that later or making yourself another cup of tea, or just watching five more minutes of your favorite show; it is understandable that we have been wired to avoid pain and seek pleasure. However, the perceived pain is a gateway to your healing, so why put it off?

Throughout this journey, notice your false ego persona resisting and know that you can still do what needs to be done by accepting your thoughts, feelings, and emotions. Keep yourself in action. Every time you up-level, resistance shows up, take it as a good sign and move forward.

I created this book to help you reclaim your power by mastering yourself, and by doing that, life will become more abundant, creative, and fulfilling for you. You will respond rather than react from your distorted, fragmented self.

To get the most out of this journey, embody these six qualities: honesty, compassion, consistency, perseverance, commitment and patience. These will help you stay on the path to expanding the self.

Get two journals dedicated to this book, as I will ask you to write in them (get your free power starter kit from my website). You will do this to enable you to open up the channels between the subconscious mind and the conscious mind.
Block out a time, a specific time of the day, when you will read this book (personally I love reading books in the morning before my day starts; it primes my day). You will be given exercises that help you unlearn your false ego persona. Reading alone will not help; studies show that within 48 hours, 80% of the information one reads is forgotten; however, when taking part in the exercises, you create an experience. Experiences expand the consciousness, leading to your higher self. Once you expand, you cannot go back.

The solution to suffering is not through the intellect, but through experience.

I wish you much success on your inner journey.

MY DAD THE HERO

My dad suffered from manic depression, also known as bipolar disorder. He had good days and bad days, but I mostly remember the bad days. This affected me on various levels that I did not comprehend at the time. I had accepted Dad lashing out by throwing things around the flat or shouting at us as normal behavior. I thought that was normal. I thought that was life.

I recall in our flat in Paris, the little eight-year-old girl trying to defend Mum from Dad; his lashing out was his way of saying that he was in pain. He sought help, but the most common way to treat mental illness in those days was through pills. He had received a Band-Aid rather than a solution to the root of his suffering. He held onto so much pain that that had been inflicted upon him.

He had misunderstandings, and not having the education to address his mental illness led him to a destructive path. The doctors handled him through anti-depressants that suppressed his emotions and wounds, which manifested as rage, blame and hurting himself and others.

I was 19 when Dad ended it all. The poor soul could not cope any longer. I was studying at an Art College in South London at the time, and I remember it all too well.

It was March 1999, and upon leaving college for the day, I waved at my friends, oblivious to what was waiting for me at home. I hopped on the 35 bus carrying my oversize A1 portfolio; I had just finished screen printing, and I reeked of the solvent-based inks. As I walked through my door, I found my aunt, two cousins, Mum, and my sister all in the living room. My initial thought was, *What the hell is going on?* As I negated the news, the words 'not my Dad' kept swirling around through my head. That evening paralyzed my heart; his unresolved death pushed me over the edge.

This experience penetrated the depth of my soul, but it led me here: my Mission. I realized people should not be suffering, and there are ways to manage, resolve, reconcile with the wounds, and pain that we hold on to. So I felt called to help people and point to a solution to suffering.
Unfortunately, suffering is a hard choice, but a choice that society has presented as 'normal.'
Suffering occurs when you have not realized your true self, your higher self; you are bound to the false ego persona created by your programming, limiting beliefs that keep perpetuating who you are not, causing a disconnect to the true self.

Suffering, unfortunately, is a choice.

Desires lead to suffering, desires from the false ego persona. However, we can transmute them by shifting our perspective, seeing them for what they really are. The root of every desire wants to awaken the self. Do not get stuck on the suffering, but shift your perspective to see what lies beyond the desires. We all have been impacted in life. Some may have had harder childhoods than others; however, all are valid, and our job now is to be accountable, responsible for who we are and how we show up in life.

We are all collectively wounded, something most of us do not wish to admit, and that is ok. The biggest wound is the separation itself from the Divine Consciousness, God or source, not remembering who we are. Being in this body places a separation between us and the invisible world. We all have forgotten our true nature; most of us do not feel whole; there is always something not quite right with us.

Can you relate to this? Ponder this for a moment before you go on to the next paragraph.

My dad seemed disconnected from his higher self, and his false ego persona had taken over his life and mine for decades. I had to unlearn, and I am still unlearning, all that does not serve me; I had to feel and still feel my way through, battle my inner demons, and slay the dragon to attain my golden fleece. Does all this sound like you? If it does, perfect; this work is challenging but know you can do this. There is a reason you are here reading this book.

I urge you to take back your power by assessing where you are not holding yourself accountable. Write in your journal (be raw and authentic) where you are giving your power away. Anytime you are a victim to your circumstances, you are giving your power away. Be accountable for your state of being. Align with your higher self; most of us act out from the inner child who wants to be seen, or wishes to express itself. Think of a time you may have possibly acted like a child, for instance, you did not get your way, and you reacted, wanting to be seen. I know I did, and she still comes up. However, with self-awareness, I tend to her needs rather than ignore her. I will explore the inner child (re-parenting yourself) later in the book.

Note that awareness plays a big part in this journey, as 90% of it brings healing—reconciliation if you like. By being aware of your wounds, you have a choice whether to respond or react.

Do you wish to react to the same old patterns that keep showing up in life, leaving you depleted, or do you want to take back your power by responding?

As previously mentioned, empowerment is not about a power pose, faking it until you make it or being bulletproof; empowerment is unlearning all that has been created by your false ego persona. It is about seeing through the illusion that has been presented to you, questioning it and asking yourself if it is true for you. Power is Creation, and you are here to realize who you really are; with that comes a raw, authentic power. The moment you align with your higher self, your true self, is the moment you declare you are a co-creator, creating a life of your own at will.

Remembrance of the self is power.

This is about reclaiming your life and being the captain of your ship. You are your own authority, and you can do so by doing the inner work. I have been doing this for years, and I am still doing it; it is an ongoing process. It has become a way of rediscovering and understanding the 'self.'

The beginning of this path seemed like torture, I cannot lie to you, but I feel I now have more control in my life. Sure, there are days I lapse, wallowing in victimhood, but my attitude to life gets me back on the horse. I learn from the descending timeline, and take the gifts with me back into the ascending timeline. With that, I feel more empowered, stronger and more certain of myself. Regardless of what shows up, I have that self-trust and resilience that helps me navigate life mostly with expansion, ease and grace. Ten percent of me that still struggles serves me as long as I transmute the 'perceived pain.'

You are not here to be perfect. Embrace your imperfections on the verge of perfection. It is all a dance, really; it is not about the ultimate destination, but becoming the highest expression. The nature of the Divine Consciousness expands, evolves; it is a dance of stillness and dynamism. So flow with the Divine Consciousness and be in a state of growth and expansion.

Expansion of the Self is love, and that is all there is: Love.

I want that for you because once upon a time; I was the one who kept giving my power away, who lost herself to relationships, who was emotionally and mentally abused, and being in that place was a nightmare, hurtful, and seemingly hopeless. However, it took me on a self-discovery path, unlearning most of what I had been taught and realizing that I had been the one getting in my own way.

Choice is the most potent act.

We all make choices in life, but how often do you make a choice aligned with your higher self, the true self?

Are you living the life that you have always wanted?

Do you make choices because someone or something told you to, or because you have been taught that way?

Do the choices you make really come from you?

I am asking you these questions because many of us make choices based on what we have been taught; we have been fed information, and most of us do not question it. We accept the reality that has been given to us, thus making choices based on that reality, but is that really true for you?

Reclaiming your power is choosing for yourself and not based on society, culture, parents, caregivers, etc.

Ask yourself and write in your journal.

What do you really want?
Where do you really want to live?
What is your passion and purpose in life?
What makes you feel alive?

Reclaiming your power is realizing you have a choice in life that is not based on scarcity, but knowing that you are a co-creator who chooses their life consciously. This is all about unlearning things that have limited you, letting go of the false ego persona and aligning with your higher self, your true self, and with that, you realize you are a co-creator who can create a life at will that is true for you.

So are you ready to do the inner work?

SELF-RESPONSIBILITY

The first step is taking 100% responsibility: Be accountable for your state of being, no matter what.

What does taking 100% responsibility mean?

'There are conditioned responses to patterns... all of that is valid, all of that is stored in your being.
The question is: How can I take responsibility of clearing that from my reality?
Once you've let go of the victim mentality... I am ready to step into who I am as a sovereign woman, as the creator of my own reality.' - Alice Bracegirdle, Founder of Bellyfit®.

I thought I had always taken 100% responsibility in my life, but it came to a point where I really had to take an honest look at myself. I did not like my reality, and I knew it was down to me to change it. The false ego persona can be devious; it will justify falsehood. It will soothe you into thinking that you are right. This restricted perspective keeps you in a loop time and time again, and you find yourself in similar situations dressed in different spouses, jobs, friends, or acquaintances.
The moment I truly began being honest with myself was the moment I began shifting my life. I realized excuses and blame kept

me in the victimhood state, and I continually kept giving my power away.

Taking responsibility means taking ownership of your actions and choices. It is about being accountable for your well-being or state and blaming no one and nothing. Being accountable for your life will lead you to a powerful, empowered state of being. You have the power to create a life that you wish, but before you do that, you first need to call all your energy, your power back to you by taking 100% responsibility.

You are not your thoughts, feelings and emotions; however, you are responsible for your actions and choices in life. Your model of reality, your inner state, comprises the actions and choices you take on every day. Note your choices impact the quality of your life, so choose according to your higher self.

The results you currently have today are from the actions you have taken in the past. If you wish for different results, take different actions. By that, I mean taking actions aligned with your higher self, your true self, rather than the false ego persona. The victimhood state is your false ego persona (that is not you); it is based on survival mode, a construct of your limiting beliefs and ancestral wounds.
So I urge you to step into your power by taking 100% responsibility in life. Every time you blame the weather, your job, your spouse, your family, you are out of alignment with your higher self.
Try to pause when you are in the heat of the moment of blaming the world. I recognize it is challenging, and I will give you a tool to achieve that pause later in the book. This will take work and practice.

The moment you blame, you give your power, your energy away. Call back your energy, reclaim your power and keep assessing what and why you are blaming the external for. Notice your emotions; what are they really saying? What is the real underlying issue? Is it really about the job or your partner? Is it your frustration that you know you can be your own authority but still blame your parents for your upbringing? Perhaps you blame your partner for not taking care of your needs, when really it is you who has abandoned yourself in order to feel loved. Whenever you blame, try to pause;

set a time when you can really assess what is going on and dig deep into the underlying issue. Get curious, write it out, and be like a detective, searching for the root of the problem. What is the actual issue?

Once you have that in hand, that awareness alone puts you back in the driver's seat; you have reclaimed your power and your energy. So I urge you throughout this journey to take 100% responsibility. As you evolve, you will find it easier to be accountable for your state of being, so be relentless with the inner work and yet still kind to yourself.

The 90-Day Plan

To ensure my coaching clients get significant results, I work with them from three months (90 days) to six months (180 days). This allows them to experience a significant change or transformation. I want that for you.
I want you to dive deep in doing the inner work and achieve the desired results; the results depend on you. It is up to you whether you do the work, commit to it and stay consistent.

When doing the inner work, I can tell you the more effort you put in, the more you will get out of it, but I also want you to pay attention to life and its rhythm. Some things may take weeks, months or years to heal, and that is ok; embrace all life as it is. There is no rush; you are always on time.
This 90-day plan is just a head start; it is not a finish line. It is a process for you to get into the habit of addressing your inner world.

Get an oversized calendar and a journal (or get your *free power starter kit*); this will be your 90-day plan. The 90-day calendar is a tracker, so you can measure your progress. What you measure, you improve on. As an example, if your aim is to tone up, you would start off weighing yourself on the scale, taking measurements of your body, or perhaps taking pictures of your body to see the result or progress. Tracking and measuring your progress will motivate you to keep going and move forward.

Get your 90-day calendar printed before reading further and purchase or make your 90-day journal.
Write every single action that you take for the next 90 days; see the following steps.

Step 1.
Write in your journal where you are in life, your state of being, and where would you like to be in 90 days. What result would you like to experience?

Step 2.
Set the intention of the desired result.
Intentions are powerful and carry you toward your goals.
Close your eyes. Sit with your intention for a few minutes once you have it (do it once).

Step 3.
Every day, write all the actions in your 90-day calendar, for example, Day 1 - Read book, Day 2 - Read book, wrote in the journal, Day 3 - Read book, self-care ritual, wrote in the journal, and carried out exercises, and so on (spend five minutes).

Step 4.
Every day, write in your 90-day journal any observations, your state of being, your feelings, your experiences of that day (spend five or ten minutes).

Step 5.
Every day, also write your progress; it can even be reading the book or writing in your journal what you are grateful for concerning this work. This step will help you stay committed and consistent, and you will certainly feel good about it. Note gratitude releases dopamine and serotonin, responsible for our emotions (spend five minutes).

Step 6.
When you have completed the book, write where you are in life after the 90 days: your state of being, any changes within yourself, your growth, how you feel and any other experiences (do it once).

THE FOUR COMPONENTS

Doing the inner work helped me develop the following four components, which I believe you also will throughout this journey: *self-awareness, clarity, empowerment and growth.*

Now let us delve into the four components:

Awareness (Self-Awareness)
Clarity
Empowerment
Growth (Evolution)

The tools that I will introduce in this book will help you become self-aware. With that awareness, you will realize your true self, your higher self; you will gain clarity and see things for what they really are, not through your filters. In doing so, you will clear out the old fragmented self, the false ego persona, and the clearer you become, the clearer your vision in life will be. The more you know what you want and do not want, the more you will feel empowered in your choices. You will feel certain about yourself, which will unleash your self-trust.

By trusting yourself, you naturally radiate confidence. Please note that many teachings push you to be confident; it is not about being confident, but how well you trust yourself and when it comes down to it, whether you can count on yourself. If yes, then that self-trust can take you anywhere in life and help you face adversity with ease and grace.

All of this is a practice for life; it is not about doing the work for 90 days and then forgetting about it; this work is for you to keep and practice daily. Stay committed and consistent, and you will grow and evolve into the true self, the higher self that you have always been but just forgotten along the way. It is your birthright to be at your fullest potential, not a slave to your false ego persona.

THE FOUNDATION

The foundation of all this is self-trust, trusting yourself; without it, you cannot really flow in life. It took me years to embody this, and when I did, it resolved stubborn issues. That one insight solved most of my problems, if you like (you will need to embody self-trust), and reconciled the powerless aspect of myself. Trusting yourself is the connection to your higher self. Without self-trust, self-doubt, unworthiness, low self-esteem, etc. creep in. Self-trust is lost when you deny yourself, your intuition, your choices in life, and ultimately when you give your power away.

To embody self-trust, you will first need to be entirely honest with yourself—raw self-honesty.
Pause a moment and really think about why being entirely honest with yourself is of the utmost importance. We've all told white lies, but those little white lies have a way of creeping in through the ego, creating patterns of falsehood.

Pause for a moment. Think of a time when you lied to justify an action or behavior to yourself. Have you ever done that? Perhaps you lie to yourself about your job, or you justify that your partner really is the person for you. They may seem innocent and harmless, but those lies eventually build a cobweb, and soon enough, you will lose yourself in it (the ego's favorite hidden place).

As I began being really honest with myself, my life shifted some of those cobwebs. I urge you to start now with yourself and others; make it relevant (for others). There is no relevance if you blurt out your entire childhood to a stranger on a bus, so keep it relevant and be kind. There are ways of communicating that do not appear offensive if they come from the heart; most people will hear your message if you are genuine. Be completely honest, adding kindness to yourself and others.

Honoring your word and keeping your promises will also rebuild self-trust.

Every promise that you break, your subconscious mind makes a record of it, creating a habit/pattern of not honoring/following through your word. This creates incoherence within the self, resulting in a lack of trust. Coherence is needed; consistency of honoring your word and reliability build trust within the self. Self-trust is you without the fears, doubts, or unworthiness; you become unstoppable and can achieve just about anything in life. Really take the time to consider that for a moment.

Self-trust is your inner guidance, your secret weapon; without it, there is no empowered you.

Every time you tell yourself that you will do something like going to the gym and not following through, it creates a pattern of uncertainty, a lack of trust, inconsistency, and you are programming your subconscious mind that you have no self-trust. Without it, you cannot be an empowered individual, so start today by rebuilding it with those two principles: self-honesty and honoring your word.

The rest of the book and exercises will also help you rebuild the self-trust you once had, but for now, begin with those two principles.

THE UNCONSCIOUS YOU

Ninety-five percent of your life is coming from the programs of your life... the first seven years of life. Every human first seven years... is downloaded to hypnosis; the brain of a child under seven is in a lower vibrational frequency... a child below seven has a lower vibration than consciousness. It's called Theta... Theta is imagination... also hypnosis. - Dr Bruce Lipton

To paraphrase Dr Bruce Lipton, your subconscious mind holds 95% of the early years in your life, your childhood. Your life is unconsciously based on programming you downloaded as a child. When you reach the age of seven, you are at the theta brainwave level, which is hypnosis (and imagination), and that aspect of the mind is more receptive, meaning children are very susceptible to behaviors, traumas, wounds—anything, really—up to the age of seven. Most of us, if unaware, react to life from those programs. I recommend you read *The Biology of Belief: Unleashing the Power of Consciousness, Matter & Miracles* by Bruce H. Lipton, Ph.D. where you can also learn about epigenetics.

Epigenetics is the study of cellular and physiological traits, or the external and environmental factors, that turn our genes on and off, and in turn, define how our cells actually read those genes. It works to see the true potential of the human mind, and the cells in our body. Bruce H. Lipton, Ph.D.

'Epigenetics: The New Science of Self-Empowerment.'

The Biology of Belief: Unleashing the Power of Consciousness, Matter & Miracles by Bruce H. Lipton, Ph.D.

The inner work is to help you upgrade your programming -- your software, if you like. Your mind is like a computer that needs a software update; it can run on the old software, but it will struggle. When people struggle, it is mostly because they are still holding on to old programming, carrying limitations for themselves.

My first memory of being criticized by Dad was when I was around six; it was over homework. I felt scared and foolish, and just wanted to hide. Those prime incidents formed a limiting belief that I was not good enough. It took me over three decades to recognize that I was sabotaging areas of my life with this limiting belief.

Unlearning your programs that limit you will take a while, but you can begin by being aware of this now. Your attitude to life ultimately is your behavior based on your programming.

How would you describe your behavior?

Start building self-trust, thus creating supportive programming and behaviors. Do not let your subconscious mind, your old programming, run the show; update your programming by doing the inner work, tend to the weeds in your mind, and plant seeds to support or enhance your life.

Today, take two actions: one, be honest with yourself (you could start writing in your journal) and two, honor your word (keep your promises).

Remember, building self-trust is critical; take action today.

The coherence of Mind and Body is the key to unclogging that full potential within yourself, balancing the mind and body, thus creating a clear connection to your soul, becoming/realizing the higher self. Keep embodying self-trust and get the mind and body balanced. When the body is low on energy (low/dense/gross vibration), the mind takes over, and you will find yourself primarily in your head.

You can test this by assessing your day. How often are you fully aware of the present moment, aware of your body? When your body is in its prime state, your energy levels are higher/subtle, and your energy flows more easily.

Your Prana, Chi or life force energy does not quite flow in your vessel if the body is clogged up with stagnant energies, stagnant emotions. The more Prana, Chi or life force energy one has, the more the body and mind can work coherently, and the more you can be the captain of your ship, your life.

The mind can be a servant to the body if you work on your life force energy and limiting beliefs. At the moment, your energy most probably depletes itself on defending your self-image, false ego persona built on wounds and traumas. How often do you defend your self-image throughout the day? Every time you want to be right or to make a point according to your false ego persona, you deplete your precious life force energy. Is it really worth your energy?

Value your Prana, Chi or life force energy more, and the less distorted your emotions and the fewer stagnant or clogged up energies you will have in your body.

Emotions are energy in motion/movement.

Admitting to others and yourself when you are in the wrong will free your energy. When your ego persona is in a constant battle with work, friends, and family, it will use a fair amount of energy to be right. The false ego persona loves to be right and takes things personally. Accepting your flaws makes you authentic and open to feedback. Life is a mirror and reflects your inner world, what you judge, what you think and what you perceive as truth.

Start questioning and doubt your limiting beliefs. Are they really true?

At the moment, there are nearly eight billion people on this planet, and they all have their own personal beliefs; they see truth as their beliefs. Scientists first believed there was only one galaxy, and they have now concluded that they exist in the hundreds, but what if in 50 years they find out they are in the thousands? Truth is variable— well, at least what I am referring to is relative truth. There are absolute truths that cannot change, but relative truth depends on perception. The absolute truths are non-changing, and the relative truth is changeable.

We live life within absolute (limitless) and relative truths (limited). Our model of reality is all about our perception; you really see the world as you are. What do you believe? What is your truth? Make the Truth work for you.

Over time, your truths will change and evolve, so be flexible; you do not have to hold on to them if they limit you. Dispose of them when they are not working for you; allow the beliefs or truths to support you in your growth, expand your consciousness and remember in seeing your wholeness as you once believed.

THE CROWN

What does it mean to take back your power? Ponder this for a moment and think about what it means for you. Write your thoughts in your journal.

Every time you allow someone or something to take you out of alignment with who you truly are is the moment you give your power away. Anytime you give your power away to your false ego persona is when you are telling yourself that you are a victim of life's circumstances. Anytime you use words such as 'I cannot' or 'why does it happen to me?' is the moment that you declare you are less than the Divine Consciousness. You stem from the Divine Consciousness; that is how powerful you are. Anything less is the false ego persona creating limitations, thus creating an illusion of victimhood.

In a group coaching call I once took part in, I remember the Coach asking one of the attendees 'Why do you keep giving your flower away?' She was referring to her personal power. It made my whole being tingle; it felt like my mind, body, and soul resonated with this 'truth'. Every time you give your power away, she would say, visualize a symbol and take it back. Visualizing a symbol made things so much easier in reclaiming my power.

I must tell you, once you recognize all the ancestral baggage that you carry and choose better for yourself, it is empowering. You can be happy-go-lucky, and one day an event in your life awakens you, shakes your traumas, and rises to the surface. If you do not recognize this, you become a victim, and life will keep reflecting back to you what you are vibrating. Your vibration is one with the trauma, and life cannot help but reflect that vibration back to you.

Note that your vibration is like a frequency, if you like; it is like tuning into the radio, and you can change the channel whenever you want, but most who are unaware stay on that channel and attract events, people, and situations from it. Changing your frequency is challenging, but doing the inner work changes it, and like a domino effect, it affects all areas of your life.

That night of the event, I was fearful for my friend; hence we walked her to the bus stop, and as we did, I carried that fear. Being on that frequency-vibration, a matching event occurred within that bandwidth, and for that, I am grateful, although I realize it may sound somewhat out of this world. Our conditioned self holds onto limited perspectives, but we stem from a Singular Consciousness (Divine Consciousness), and perspectives are limitless.

Be formless, limitless, expansive, and continuously evolving as the Divine Consciousness.

Isabel

Growing up, I took on the caregiver's role, and other people's needs were my priority. One way of giving your power away is making everyone else's needs more important than yours. This took a while to unlearn and perhaps one of the most significant lessons in my life.

Let us dive into making yourself a priority; some of you may think it is selfish to put oneself before others. There is selfishness, where you are egocentric, the center of the world, and benefit from others; and there is wise-selfishness, where you fill your cup first, so you then can help others. Filling your cup is a must. Without you in a full optimal state, you cannot assist others.

The extreme lesson of prioritizing my needs, filling my cup first, manifested in my late twenties, and it began with Isabel. I had come out of a relationship, nothing exciting. It was merely for the sake of being in a relationship, and eventually, we went our separate ways. I took several months to take a breather for myself, and I had come across a mainstream law of attraction book, which I no longer use. I have found other ways to manifest. Note, the law of attraction is a natural law (one of the universal laws) and applies in our day-to-day life.

Isabel felt like a dream when I first met her. Whenever I would look into her eyes, I would lose myself in awe. I felt the magic and fireworks that I sought. I wanted to attract a beautiful woman, and I did precisely that, but in my ignorance, I thought Isabel was the answer to my void or disconnect from myself.

When life presented her to me, two things came to mind; first, she was better than me because she looked more attractive than I did (that is what I told myself). The second stemmed from that misunderstanding: I had put her on a pedestal, so I naturally put myself down. Thoughts of insecurity came to me. She was too good for me, and I was unworthy of being with her. I built a limiting belief of 'not being worthy of love' stemming from 'not worthy of Dad's love.' I felt rejected repeatedly by him. The criticism, the 'not good enough' daughter, comments like 'what's wrong with you?' resurfaced with a vengeance. Dad's comments kept perpetuating unconsciously throughout my relationship. The programming had already festered into my being, and I did not realize the relationship, a person I thought I manifested on purpose, reflected my wounds. Do you think my soul guided me to her? Or my false ego persona? Either way, it brought out gifts and healing, however painful my ego perceived it to be.

Like all relationships, we went through our honeymoon phase, then the conflicts began, and the wounds blinded me, doing the best thing for me. Wounds can take over if unchecked, and we may end up thinking it is love driving us. If unaware of the relationship dynamics, we blame each other for things that do not relate to us and we cannot see that it is the wounds at play. These projections come back and forth from both parties; like a tennis game, the ball keeps going back and forth.

For example, a friend's scenario looked like this: 'Why didn't you do the dishes?' She would get angry, thinking behind that action her partner did not love her enough to do them.

It is a constant battle if both parties are unaware of these projected wounds; you are both asking for your needs to be met (needs that your parents or caregivers did not provide), and when your partner does not meet them, you think that he or she does not care for or love you.

In my earlier years, I felt obligated to meet my family's needs; I wanted them to feel better, but I began tending to their needs before mine, and that is precisely what I did with Isabel. Her needs became my priority; she needed nurturing, unconditional love, which I happily provided, but I continued with the misunderstanding that she came first, and I kept giving my power away by making myself small, irrelevant, and unimportant next to her. I began disregarding myself; it started with little things, and because I was in love, I thought that is what one did, looking after her happiness, and in return, she would look after mine.

It was all a misunderstanding in my head, really, a belief I perhaps picked up from culture, society—who knows? Still, it was a belief I took on as my own. Initially, the little things seemed irrelevant, but they built up gradually to a point where I found myself in an alarming situation and succumbed to accepting it as 'normal.'

I love working out. I love feeling healthy in my body. Before meeting Isabel, I would go to the gym three or four times a week, and I recollect one Saturday morning when she first asked me to stay with her. It seemed innocent, but it quickly escalated as I stayed in more often over my workouts, which then evolved to staying in over my friends as well. I began gaining weight, because I allowed myself to not go to the gym. We ate out a lot together, and when we stayed in, it meant pizzas, popcorn, desserts—you get the picture—so the kilos piled up. Then the criticism followed; the name-calling began. Eventually, I did not feel good about myself. So my body image was affected, and I kept giving my power away repeatedly. I kept making excuses with my friends not to go out, so I would stay in with her, and it all went downhill from there, and this was all on me. I allowed this because the wounds were too domineering. The wound of not being good enough, the fear of being criticized all presented in my reality. I was reliving my childhood environment.

The relationship worsened, and Isabel left me for another. The wound of abandonment reared its head, fragmenting every piece of my mind, body and soul. I had become so small, so powerless, and self-pity became my ally. I was in denial and believed I could get her back, throwing away my self-respect and self-love to regain the 'illusion of love.' Love did not drive me to disgrace, but rather the desperation of not wanting to feel abandoned. The relationship had drained the soul out of me but led me to my self-discovery path. I finally began my healing process (reconciling - bringing the wounds to awareness/light), and to this day, I am truly am grateful.

It took several years to transmute the pain and finally turn it into my purpose, my Mission, and reclaim the power I had given away. Being in your power means having so much love for yourself in a non-egotistical manner. It means having self-respect for yourself, and with that, you radiate beauty from your heart and your solar plexus. In Sanskrit, they describe the third chakra, the solar plexus, as the City of Jewels. So treat your City of Jewels with utter respect. Use your experiences, your lessons, and turn them into gifts. Knowing that you are more than your wounds and traumas, see the bigger picture; connect the dots to what life is showing you. Your life is a mirror of your inner world. When the external offers you something not to your liking, ask yourself what is going on internally?

Know that you are a magnificent and beautiful being on the verge of your rebirth. You have the key within you at all times; you have the power to change your life and be a Rose. Radiate your beauty without force. People in life will mishandle you, and acceptance is critical in all this. With acceptance, you can choose better, and that is what empowerment is all about—having the choice for your highest good with full awareness instead of entertaining other people's projections. You have the option not to take on their wounds. You get to stand in your power in the most loving and honorable way by staying in your center and remaining grounded

like a tree; when there is a storm, allow your branches to bend, but you firmly stay planted, rooted, whilst keeping your crown.
Not everyone will understand you, and other times, your behavior and actions may change; your loved ones may feel this and say you have changed; take it as a compliment; that means you are evolving. Some loved ones may understand you, and some may not accept them as they are, and if friends disappear, that may be due to your vibration frequency changing. Some people you are connected with may be trauma-based, and when healing occurs, those traumas that once connected to those people may naturally fall off once you address them, or you may not resonate with them anymore. It may happen or not; people may grow with you as you evolve.

Resist nothing in life; what you resist persists, which is all ego-based; your false ego persona will fight to stay where it is most comfortable. ACCEPT WHAT IS. The self-image that you have built over the years will disintegrate and take form as the higher self, your true self. The more you let go, the more you will remember who you are.

The Key to this is Acceptance.

KEEPING YOUR CROWN

I hope you have a better idea of the 'symbolic crown,' the importance of meeting your needs (filling your cup first), and being the person you are meant to be, a Rose. Now let us get to work on how you would practically keep your 'symbolic crown' (if you have not done so, please pick a symbol). The way I achieved this took me decades. I went through so much pain, but in the end, it was worth it, and I came through the other side. Do not take this the wrong way—many times, thoughts came across my mind (and still do) that were disempowering, and those thoughts you cannot control; see them like the weather. Accept them and let them pass through. It is important to not attach meanings to them; thoughts have little power unless they fuse with emotions and feelings. It took me ages to practice and refine to a comfortable stage, so this inner work you are doing takes daily practice and refinement. However, the results are satisfying. Having self-awareness and choosing the response from an empowered state is very liberating. Being led by your wounds without your awareness, not knowing why you act in a certain way throughout your life, is not a life but enslavement in a mental prison. It may sound harsh, but I want you to understand that doing the inner work frees you, and you will end up asking yourself why you did not do it sooner. I know I did; I wish I had known all of this a decade ago, but I realized the Divine is always on 'time.'

Write in your journal.

1. When do you give your power away? Work, spouse, partner, family, friends?

2. What do you do when you give it away? People-please? Make yourself small so others feel comfortable around you?

3. Write in detail your thoughts, feelings, emotions, and any stories that come up for you. For example, perhaps the story is if I am a 'good' person, people will like me (people-pleasing).

4. Do you believe your thoughts and the stories you tell yourself? If not, go to the next question. If yes, ask yourself why. Keep asking yourself why until you no longer wish to hold on to your current thoughts, feelings, emotions, and stories. Dig deep and get to the root.

5. Do you wish to hold on to your current thoughts, feelings, emotions and stories? If not, move on to the next question; if yes, keep asking yourself why until you no longer wish to hold on to your current thoughts, feelings, emotions, and stories. Dig deep and get to the root.

6. What thoughts, feelings, and emotions would you like to experience? Write them down.

7. Write a new story you wish to experience. For example, I want to date someone who sees my wholeness or work where I am valued. Get specific.

8. Finally, ask yourself what practical steps you could take to embody and support your new story. For example, I will look into working at a workplace that values its employees.

9. Make a plan (action-oriented) based on those practical steps.

10. Take action.

Congratulations on completing the work.

Time for a declaration now.

Place both hands on your heart chakra and say aloud five times—
DECLARE IT with CONVICTION:

I AM A POWERFUL CO-CREATOR, CREATING AN ABUNDANT
AND FULFILLING LIFE. SO BE IT, SO IT IS.

If this declaration does not resonate with you, create one of your
own. Listen to your Inner Guidance—you always know best—and
come up with one along the line that you are a co-creator with
positive attributes and use 'I AM.' These two words are most potent
and create whatever you choose. I manifest with the words 'I AM,'
especially when writing them down. 'So Be It, So It Is' seals the
declaration. Choose your Declarations carefully and always for your
highest good and the highest good of all. When co-creating your
life, always do it for your highest good and the highest good of all.

LOOK AFTER YOUR MUM

How could such an innocent sentence have so much power? When Mum and Dad divorced, we moved from Paris to London. He had become significantly unbalanced. It was supposed to be a Christmas holiday. I was around 9 or 10 years old before Mum decided we would all spend Christmas in London with our Auntie and cousins. It was Dad, Mum, my sister and me with the family in London. What was a festive season turned out to be a significant point in my life, and little did I know one event could change everything. Dad had drunk that night, and all hell broke loose. He had driven Mum to her limit. That was the last straw.

Whilst chaos was perpetuating through my mind and body, Mum asked me the ultimate question that changed my entire life: 'Do you want to live in London?' I paused and answered simply, 'Yes.' I struggled to live in London, to begin with, as it seemed so different from what I had previously known. It took me years to settle in. I remember doubting myself wondering and if it had been the right decision. Connecting the dots, it made sense.

Dad moved to the north of France, and we used to visit him by using the Ferry from Portsmouth to Calais; it was a rather fun adventure. I loved sleeping in the cabin overnight and waking up to the enigmatic sea. I would gaze out the window and observe the waves of the ocean with profound curiosity, forgetting briefly who I was. Dad often wrote letters, and to this day, there are still a few I hold close to my heart. One of them said, 'Look after Mum; you are a big girl now.' I was about 11- 12 years old, and I remember Dad telling me a few times before to look after her. Well, I took on that responsibility seriously; it felt right, but it was a heavy burden for me at that age. I felt responsible, and I had not even hit puberty yet. A long journey began of unlearning, not meeting my own needs. It was rooted within me, deeply ingrained.

The limiting belief that others' needs are more important than mine showed up through my romantic relationships. It had its benefit according to my false ego persona, keeping me small and invisible. All limiting beliefs have benefits, a deep-rooted desire. The desire for me was 'safety;' not being visible meant I was safe from harm. I hid from Dad to not get shouted at or criticized. So as long as I kept my head down, I felt safe, and that limiting belief took form to protect me as a child, but growing up, it manifested as pain and sabotage in life. It may sound strange to you that limiting beliefs have somewhat of a benefit, a deep-rooted desire. However, the false ego persona builds them to keep you away from the pain you experienced as a child. While it creates such programs, it also keeps you in a limiting state, as they root in survival. The false ego persona will not help you go beyond your mind and achieve your fullest potential. It is a program, and that is its job. Your job is to be aware of it and choose consciously from your higher self, your true self, your empowered state.

Have you ever notice repeated patterns in life, knowing that it is not for your highest good (relationships, jobs, etc.)? Can you think back to a time?

Your limiting beliefs will consume you, create never-ending stories, make your head spin, tell you the same thing repeatedly, justify why it is right for you. The issue for me was that I feared Isabel would leave me if I did not abide by her needs; I felt she was better than me; I handed over my worth to her; and the fear of abandonment kept me in a state of victimhood. Deep down, I knew the relationship was not right for me; I had lost myself and depended on her validation and acceptance. I had little power to myself, and finally, when the breakup took place, the Divine smiled at me whilst I cried in vain.

It is critical for you to meet your own needs; you cannot expect your partner, mum, daughter, son, friends or anyone really to meet your needs. It is your responsibility, and anyone consciously willing to meet your needs is a bonus. Some of you may disagree on this, but believe me, expecting others to meet your needs will repeatedly disappoint you. We are flawed human beings, and with that imperfection on the verge of perfection, everyone in your life at one point will disappoint you, and that is more than ok. You cannot control the actions or behaviors of others, but you can undoubtedly control yours. People will always disappoint you according to your expectations. It is not fair to them or to you. So meeting your needs is a must, and remember: If people meet your needs, take it as a bonus, and if you have specific needs, have the conversation first with them and come to an agreement.

Write in your journal.

Emotional/ Mental/ Behavioral Needs
Physical/ Energy Needs
Spiritual Needs

Write in your journal.
How can you meet those needs for each category?

We will explore further; however, for now, list your initial view on how you would meet them.

Meeting your own needs will empower you, and you will gain more control of the self. You will not feel so dependent on people or yearn for others to meet them. Another bonus, you will also refuel yourself and tend to your life force energy, giving you an extra boost. You will be in your higher power and on a higher/subtle vibration, making it much easier to connect to the higher self. When you are low in energy, you will most probably find yourself irritable, angry, frustrated, stressed or anxious.
Have you ever found yourself in those states? The less energy you have, the more you are rooted in the false ego persona. So meeting your needs has a lot of benefits. Let us explore further how to meet your needs.

THE THREE DIMENSIONS

EMOTIONAL NEEDS

For clarification, the dimension of emotional needs covers mental and behavioral needs as well. Emotions affect your thoughts (mental) and how you act (behavioral). All three come as a package if you like, and the order of them expressing themselves may differ. The thought may come first, or some may argue it is the emotion first; regardless, they all come as one package. This dimension is classed as 'the Emotional Needs'.

The first step in all this is awareness; what beliefs or thoughts are holding you hostage?

Exercise

For the next 24 hours, I would like you to observe your main thoughts like a witness, a neutral observer, meaning without judgment (judgment will only create an emotional charge). Write them down on the go, or use your smartphone if easier.

Then go through them and try to see if there is a pattern.

Are there thoughts that may repeat more than others? Perhaps it may sound something like this throughout your day: I am not doing enough; what if my boss does not think it is good enough, or what if the dinner is not good enough for my family? Do you see the pattern here?

The pattern would be 'not good enough.' Since this a limiting belief that once crippled me, it may sound obvious; it stems from 'I am not good enough.'

Collect as much information as you can. Be like a detective when observing your thoughts that keep repeating the same song.

If you procrastinate, do not worry; that is resistance kicking in, the fear-based ego trying to put up a fight. Acknowledge it, thank it for sharing its concern and take action. Try your best to remain neutral.

Action minimizes fear.

Now that you have figured it out, write your limiting belief in your journal in the Emotional needs section.

This is something that you seek, and most probably seek it from the external, possibly from work, spouse, partner, friends or family members, so you would feel 'good enough.' It has nothing to do with them, do you see that? It has everything to do with you, and the good news is that you have the choice to do something about it. Once you have that limiting belief, find the hidden benefit.

In my case, the notion of not doing enough kept me in a state of overwork. Overworking would numb that limiting belief; hence I was not aware of it and its pain. All limiting beliefs help deter pain, a coping mechanism, which is normal; however, now you must upgrade your operating system with supported beliefs. The 'not enough' limiting belief prioritized work over my well-being. I was filling a void, numbing the noise that constantly kept repeating itself, holding onto a misunderstanding that my work related to my worth.

By recognizing the hidden benefit, you can now question the limiting belief and ask yourself if that is true for you. Question all your limiting beliefs and keep asking yourself if they are true. By creating new beliefs that support you, you will create 'new truths.' Make sure that these truths enhance your growth in your personal and professional life. The glorious thing about this work is you can program your subconscious mind with any beliefs you desire, given that you have addressed the limiting beliefs first.

The next step

Now that you have your limiting belief, reframe it to something that will support you. For example, the new supportive belief/truth for me evolved to 'I am more than enough.' Make it personal. It has to feel right within you, a new truth for you. This process can be repeated as many times as you like, as you may have other limiting beliefs you may hold on to.

You will naturally behave differently the more than you tend to your needs; you will appreciate and love yourself, and feel more gratitude in life. When we express gratitude, our brain releases Dopamine and Serotonin, the two crucial neurotransmitters responsible for our emotions, making us feel good. They enhance our mood immediately, making us feel happy from the inside. Feeling good can affect the other dimensions, the physical and spiritual, like a domino effect. You may feel like going to the gym or eating something healthy; perhaps instead of procrastinating your meditation, you may feel like doing it, as you feel happier. When happiness becomes your set point, the world is your oyster. With the practice of nourishing your needs (all three), you will feel more empowered within yourself.

While you do this, please do not misunderstand and become an extremely self-reliant person who never accepts help or is afraid to ask for help. Keep it all in balance. This is about becoming a self-reliant, self-sufficient individual and yet open to kindness, generosity and love. The point is to show you the importance of filling your cup first. Have beautiful, healthy, loving relationships without wearing the small print on your sleeve: 'Please look after my needs.'

Once you have come up with a new belief, you must reinforce it by introducing activities or actions that support it, for example, in my case for 'I am more than enough,' I would treat myself to a massage, going to the spa, getting a haircut—the list goes on. So find activities or actions to reinforce your new belief. Also, think of practical scenarios; when having this new belief, think about how you will relate it to work, friends, colleagues, etc. I took rest when needed, especially when working; I placed healthy boundaries with people; and I learned to say no to things that were not for my highest good.

In the Emotional needs, you will also need to manage your emotions by being aware of the four hormones and neurotransmitters that need regulating on a day-to-day basis. Overall, these four chemicals will stabilize your mood, and you will feel balanced. Please do not skip this part, as your emotions affect the other dimensions of the physical/energy and the spiritual. Find ways of incorporating the four hormones/chemicals *moderately* and write them down.

Serotonin
Dopamine
Endorphins
Oxytocin

Serotonin: a hormone and a neurotransmitter thought to regulate anxiety, happiness, and mood. Overall, it makes you feel balanced.

Meditation
Yoga
Sun exposure/Vitamin D
Going for a run
Deep breathing (diaphragmatic)
Omega-3 fatty acids

Dopamine: a hormone and a neurotransmitter. Motivation hormone, released when you experience pleasure and reward.

Gratitude
Celebrating small wins
Finishing a task
Music
Exercises
Hugging your pet
Getting enough sleep
Avocados/Nuts

Endorphins trigger a positive feeling and reduce the perception of pain released when exercising.

Exercise
Laughter
Dancing
Meditation
Dark Chocolate
Getting a massage

Oxytocin is a peptide hormone and neuropeptide. It is known as the 'Love Hormone' or 'Cuddle Chemical,' also released through social bonding.

Sun exposure/Vitamin D
Hugging family or friends
Empathy for others
Playing with a pet
Holding hands

PHYSICAL NEEDS

The physical needs intertwine with emotional needs. As you look after your body, your energy levels are higher; the lower your energy, the more distorted your emotions become. So it is vital for you not to skip this dimension. Please consult a doctor if you are not fit to exercise or have health-related issues.

Write in your journal.

Engage in various exercises that you enjoy, such as resistance exercises, walking, jogging, yoga, martial arts, dancing—the list goes on. Note you will do this every single day for at least 30 minutes, no less. Do not push yourself too hard. Listen to your body and yet challenge yourself, always in balance. If you feel extra tired, perhaps a walk will suffice, or if you have extra energy, you could do resistance/strength training.

I will leave it up to you. Write your daily exercises/activities.

Nourishment—how do you nourish yourself? I invite you to write what you eat on average and assess yourself. Is it healthy for you? Nutrition is personal, so I invite you to do your research and aim for a well-balanced, healthy diet. Consult a nutritionist if needed. Aim to eat to enhance your energy. Be honest with yourself and set out a weekly nourishment plan.

Do you drink enough water? Hydration is important. Do your research and consult a doctor or nutritionist if needed. Again, this is personal. Some may need to drink more water than others. Do your research. Write how many glasses you plan to drink per day and follow through.

I will dive into self-care activities later in the book.

Your body is your temple. Treat it with love and respect.

SPIRITUAL NEEDS

This dimension is about connecting to the Divine Consciousness, God, Source—whatever term you use. It is about connecting to something much bigger than yourself, believing in something you may not comprehend. It could connect to your higher self or soul, or you may just feel or sense something out there; perhaps it is energy.

If this does not resonate, do not worry. Skip this section (or do breath work) and proceed with the other two dimensions.
For the spiritual dimension, write ways you can connect to that Source. Is it through meditation, prayer, chanting? In what ways can you connect to that higher power?

THE HIGHER POWER WEEKLY RITUAL

Now that you have written all the activities down, from all three dimensions, create your *Higher Power Weekly Ritual* by printing out a blank weekly calendar (or get your free power starter kit). Write when and where you will perform your activities (block out times) throughout the day for the Emotional, Physical and Spiritual dimensions. Be specific, as it will be easier for you to follow through. Remember the benefits of nourishing those needs.

Upon rising and just before you fall asleep, visualize yourself as an empowered individual. See yourself feeling strong in your body, in your mind, and connect to your inner guidance and Source every single day. This will enable you to get the best results, as this will address your subconscious mind.

You access the theta brain frequency during those times, just after you wake up and before you fall asleep. This state, as mentioned before, is hypnosis, rapid programming, and those are the best times to reprogram your subconscious mind to your pleasing. I urge you to use all five senses when doing this; your subconscious mind does not know what is real and not. The more you implement this, the easier it will be to follow through with the activities.

Introducing the empowered version of yourself in your mind using all the five senses will make it easier for you. Have fun with it. Use music and/or essential oils, print out visuals, get creative, tune into your inner guidance, and see what you come up with.

A tip that helps me when I do not feel like carrying out an activity is to frame it to 'I get to' and fill in the blank: 'I get to go to the gym,' 'I get to exercise,' etc. Another tip: Do not over-think; just take action. In time, the activities will turn into habits, and before you know it, you will come to perform them every day effortlessly. That happened with my meditation practice. It was new to me, and it was hard for me to do in the beginning, but the more I practiced, the easier it became to meditate every day.

'Making a choice that is 1 percent better or 1 percent worse seems insignificant in the moment, but over the span of moments that make up a lifetime these choices determine the difference between who you are and who you could be.' - James Clear, Atomic Habits: An Easy & Proven Way to Build Good Habits & Break Bad Ones.

CONNECTION

The 'self' realizes itself the moment it goes beyond the false ego persona, when in complete absorption with Source, God, the Divine Consciousness. It is a state of Samadhi, a state of Oneness. The individual stops identifying itself with all labels and roles it has taken on.

The more the 'self' is open to Source, the Divine Consciousness, then the less of the 'I' or 'Me' there is. The more you connect to Source, the more you will realize life is not about you. I have heard so many times through Teachers, Sages, etc. that life is not about us; it is about the impact we have on others. If you are a parent, it may be easier to comprehend this through your devotion to your children, wanting the best for them, wanting them to have a meaningful or significant life. Your devotion and love for your children go beyond the false ego persona.

The moment you are in a state of pure awareness is the moment you transcend the false ego persona. I am sure you have had a glimpse of this state. Have you ever lost yourself in awe, your eyes lit up, possibly tears falling down your cheeks, and experienced so much love, happiness, or peace within yourself? That is a glimpse of self-transcendence, transcending the ego persona and experiencing yourself as the Divine Consciousness. We are part of the Divine Consciousness, and we are a speck amongst hundreds or thousands of galaxies, and we make our lives all about ourselves. I have often found myself in my head (and still do) and have had to pull myself back to the present moment. We see life through our false ego persona, and with that, we limit our life. When you genuinely believe you are a consciousness that is vast and expansive, you will allow the belief of how powerful and creative you are, a co-creator, a god or goddess.

You will see beyond yourself, beyond the mind, and with that, you will 'act' outside of 'what can I get, or what's in it for me' to 'how can I be of service to the world?' This will evolve as you do the inner work and expand your consciousness. You will realize serving others is also serving yourself, and that is the highest life you can have.

Being self-less will open up the true nature of who you are.

You may have heard of sages, monks, nuns, etc. serving for the greater good, responding to consciousness's will, if you like. You see through that act; it is a presence that comes from you, through you; you feel inspired, expansive, creative, happy, and that is all you.

In my coaching sessions, I get out of my false ego persona when I truly connect to serving my clients. I find myself a vessel to the Divine Consciousness, and it is no longer 'Stéphanie' coaching but the Higher Source/Power working/expressing through me. There are no limits to what it does. I allow it to guide me, and I never know what to expect.

We are so much more, and unfortunately, most of us have bought into the belief that we are merely a limited human being. I invite you to open your mind by releasing the false ego persona and recognize your true nature throughout this journey. Aim to be

70/80% of the higher self and 30/20% of the false ego persona, then ultimately aim for 90%/10%, and so forth. Do not become overwhelmed. Start where you feel more comfortable and escalate the percentage bit by bit. Remember, this work is for life, so take one step at a time. Doing the inner work will help you unlearn and let go of layers of conditioning and unravel a powerful multidimensional human being capable of creating a life of possibilities.

Possibilities are endless.

Service is the most sustainable way to stay connected to the Divine Consciousness. By serving, you naturally gravitate to your higher self, your true self, thus letting go of the false ego persona. As I mentioned before, the ego persona can only do limited things; it will keep you in a 'perceived comfort zone' or stay in survival mode. We are not meant to just 'survive;' we are meant to 'thrive' in life, which is our 'birthright.' Look at the sun, look at nature; they thrive and give their best to us, expecting nothing in return, being of service, honoring their roles on earth.

Our part here in life is to recognize that role and do the best we can to help people in need whilst still honoring ours. Create human connections, build communities because our connection to each other is our strength. We are all interconnected. We all have a role or place in this life. Figure it out by living and letting life impact you. There is no rush. All is perfectly designed. By covering your emotional, physical, and spiritual dimensions, you become an equipped, balanced human being, which helps you stay in your center, in your 'beingness,' and have a sense of equanimity.

Equanimity will connect you to other individuals according to that frequency, a balanced frequency, a neutral point. Please note that neutrality is not passive, weak or mindless, but an energy/frequency beyond the mind. See neutrality as a 'Unification' between the 'self' and the Divine Consciousness. This is to be experienced, not intellectually understood. The more you do the inner work, the more you will experience 'neutrality/equanimity'. Aim for that balanced frequency in life when connecting to other people. Being in that balanced frequency, the neutral point will help you connect to Source and co-create much more smoothly and with integrity.

Now that you have established that connection plays a huge part and accesses a more giant network, the Divine Consciousness, I invite you to think of us, human beings, as cells and the Divine Consciousness as a brain or whatever you envision, and for it to function, we need to work together by not identifying ourselves as the ego, but our true selves; by transcending the ego. Be the individual consciousness you are and yet still connect to the ultimate Source of all. I hope now you understand the essentiality of meeting your needs (the three dimensions) and the importance of transcending the false ego persona in order to connect essential to Source.

SPACE

If not crucial, it is vital to pause, breathe, and hear the spaces in life. Learn to pause in your busy lifestyle. For those of you who have mastered the art of slowing down, I applaud you, and I invite you to practice more frequent full awareness in your daily activities. For the 'busy bees,' you must learn to slow down. As you slow down and are fully present in the moment, time expands. Yes, you have read it correctly: Time expands. The more you are in a 'state of awareness', the more you can buy time.

Pausing throughout your day is important because it gives you the space to connect to the Divine Consciousness and your inner guidance. If you are forever busy and lost in thoughts, mindlessly performing activities, how can you connect to Source and feel your inner guidance? It is vital to quiet the 'busy' mind, and you do this by slowing down, by being present in the moment. The more present you are, the better you make choices from your higher self, not based on the false ego persona, society, friends, family, etc. Listening to your inner guidance will help you trust yourself and be more comfortable with uncertainty. Growing that self-trust within you is vital for you to be an empowered individual.
Meeting your needs in all dimensions, having self-trust and connecting to your inner guidance as needed will make you unstoppable. Imagine being so certain of yourself, having a direct, clear inner knowing guiding you at all times. To me, that is powerful, the ability to create at will with complete trust.

The next time you feel you want to rush or go faster, I urge you to pause for a moment and take ten deep diaphragmatic breaths. Once you feel calm, be fully present, whether brushing your teeth or looking for your keys, and be there in the moment. Observe what happens and what you feel. If you can, write your observations in your journal after the process. Approach this as play and experiment with it.

Keep listening to your inner guidance, connect to the Divine Consciousness, and build that self-trust and higher power within yourself. As you do that, no one or nothing can take that away from you, and that state can go anywhere with you, anytime you are aware.

STAGE 2

THE DEEPER WORK

THE WOUND OF ABANDONMENT

When I was around 2-3 years old, Mum made a tough decision for my well-being; it would be best for me to stay in London for a month. Mum was pregnant with my sister at the time, and she could not cope with both of us. She needed help and asked my Aunty and cousins to look after me for a month. In the end, I stayed a little longer, and they became like a second family.

Looking back, I tried to imagine how I must have felt like as a toddler, one minute in the arms of my mother, whom I adore, and the next in a foreign country away from her. I cannot be 100% certain if that became a trauma, but I felt it affected me dramatically. I felt loved, but I also felt abandoned, and this wound was to resurface later on in my life.

It reappeared when Dad left this physical realm; the wound reactivated itself among the grief, sorrow, and anger toward my dad for leaving us. I was angry at him for years, but I also felt guilty and ashamed for feeling that way. It was the deepest cut and, it felt like it shattered my soul into a hundred pieces. The world no longer made sense. One minute I was merely a student focusing on my studies, and the next, a violent disruptor came into play, a heavy load crushing itself on my chest, weighing me down, day by day. The first two seconds upon rising would be ignorant bliss then, once awareness kicked in, the pain would strike my heart down, gradually barricading itself with a non-penetrable wall. The simplest task would take a tremendous amount of effort. I felt like I was in a non-ending nightmare, and the only peace I would experience was in my sleep.

I felt abandoned; I felt left behind. The first couple of years were excruciating. I had to repeat a year of my degree. I could not function. I could not focus on my studies. I was an emotional mess. The abandonment goes so deep within us all, and yet most of us are unaware. This wound goes back to our ancestors, and it sneakily passes through the womb to womb, mother to child, each of us carrying this invisible torment. The abandonment wound comes from the separation of the Divine Consciousness, Source, God if you like. Without the human body, we are pure energy connected to Source. Being in a human body unaware of its origin, of its self-remembrance, creates a sense of separation, deepening the human drama and its wound of abandonment. The 'I' creates further separation from Source, and most of us grow up thinking we are just a human body, without a soul, spirit or energy. This misunderstanding creates such a deep wound, like a separation from our mother, the Essence, your Essence. Deep down, we all feel that disconnection; we seek connection and strive to reconcile with this separation.

The forgetting of not knowing your true nature is the wound itself and is the separation, but in remembrance, you feel whole; as some say healed, remember that the word derives from the Old English word haelen.

All this inner work is 'remembering who we are'.

We have forgotten our true nature, and the false ego persona is what you have developed to survive in this society. You are so much more than you perceive. Have you ever heard of something along the lines that we only use 10% of our potential? Well, that is because we identify with the persona. Letting go of the persona is the gateway to your freedom.

Let go of your pain and the overbearing wounds that cause a disconnection. Distraction deepens our disconnection; distracted with work, entertainment, drama—anything that takes you out of alignment, of who you are. Accept the cards you are presented with and make your move by remembering who we are.

It is a challenging journey in remembering who you are. Still, it is rewarding when you get a taste of inner freedom, a taste of empowerment, a taste of pure bliss. It makes it worthwhile, and the more inner work you put in, the more you shall reap the benefits, unlocking your full potential.
This work will bring out resistance; your false ego persona will battle and bring you down to stay where you are, and that is when your will needs to be stronger than your thoughts, feelings and emotions. Do not allow your ego to betray you because it will try its hardest. You are not at war with it. However, you are not its servant, so take back control and direct the mind to serve you for your highest good.

Keep remembering and keep letting go, shedding the layers of the conditioned self. I hope you have a better idea of the wound of abandonment. I encourage you to answer the questions below in your journal before heading to the next paragraph.

Contemplate and write in your journal. Be honest.

What does the wound of abandonment mean to you personally? What is your story?

Do you feel you are continually giving: spouse, partner, friends, family or work?

Do you people-please: spouse, partner, friends, family or work?

Do you put your own interests aside: spouse, partner, friends, family or work?

Do you place boundaries: spouse, partner, friends, family or work?

How do you feel throughout your day? (Do you experience guilt or shame?)

Does your mood or happiness depend on your spouse, partner, friends, family or work?

Can you be alone with your own thoughts, your company? If not, what do you and why?

Are you dependent on your relationship? Do you feel jealous or insecure often? (If you are not in a current relationship, use the last relationship you were in.)

Are you happy for your spouse or partner when he or she is doing better in life? (If you are not in a current relationship, use the last relationship you were in.)

Do you feel insecure when your spouse or partner is independent of you? (If you are not in a current relationship, use the last relationship you were in.)

Do you remain in unhealthy relationships or situations, and why? Dig deep.

Do you overwork?

Do you betray or abandon yourself over; spouse, partner, friends, family or work? Why? To be liked, loved, accepted, or to not upset others? Dig deep.

Do you speak your truth? (Truth that is relevant, compassionate and honest.)

Do you feel you are a self-reliant individual?

Do you feel you need permission from others?

Do the opinion of others matter more than yours?

Do you need validation from others?

Write any other thoughts on the subject.

I realize these questions are challenging, and I honor you for doing the work.

Contemplate and answer the questions truthfully. These questions are to bring awareness to your wound of abandonment. Therefore, the more honest you are with yourself, the more beneficial it is for you, and you can finally address what needs your full attention. By addressing the illusion of separation within the self, your entire world has the potential to look a lot different from the things you have previously settled for. We make do to feel secure in life, but that constant need for security keeps you in a limiting framework, giving you an illusion of certainty. There are no certainties, only impermanence. Impermanence (change) is all about the unknown and uncertainty. All we can do is to be certain of ourselves, which will help us face the unknown and adversity. Get comfortable and curious about the unknown. Only in the unknown can you create. Creativity is in the 'now;' the unknown is in the present moment. You are a co-creator, and you can create from a space of certainty from within, and with that, you cannot help but receive life's greatest gifts.

The wound of abandonment kept creeping up in my life because I had not addressed it; I kept avoiding it, suppressing it, and it continuously popped up through different people and situations until one day I had had enough. After Isabel had left me for another, I was left with the belief that I was not good enough, not pretty enough, not perfect enough, like there was something wrong with me. Before her, I was pretty confident, and I tried dating again, but still nothing long-lasting. If anyone got too close to my heart, I would get scared. Love was not the issue; it was the fear of my wound being reactivated. I had numbed the pain somehow, but not so successfully. The wound needed addressing; it required my care, attention, and love, but I had left it because I did not know any better. We are not taught how to address our emotions or traumas at school, but I hope they will teach us such things one day.

Do not let your unresolved wounds take over. Avoiding your unresolved wounds will eventually spread across all areas of your life. Before I reconciled an unresolved wound, it had unleashed its virus and affected my work life. Before the wound was reactivated, my work life was completely intact. It took a vast amount of effort to get my degree. My career was my priority, and somehow the virus infiltrated itself throughout my life. It attracted me to a couple of work situations where a perceived authority would project their wounds.

To summarize the story, one of the work situations felt like I had to prove myself to the distorted, masculine authority figure (father wound - rejection). In order to feel accepted and gain that validation, I had betrayed, had abandoned myself by people-pleasing, over-working, and by allowing abusive behavior from the perceived authority.

Reconcile within yourself the unresolved wounds so that people and situations are not attracted to them/to you. It is all about letting go, facing them without judgment, forgiving yourself and others for having that misunderstanding and seeing the actual reality from your higher self instead of your wounded perceptions.

Before you go on to the next chapter, make sure you have written your answers to the previous questions. The more that you are aware, the more you can make empowered, conscious choices in life.

RE-PARENTING YOUR INNER CHILD

I congratulate and honor you for coming this far.

It is time to re-parent your inner child, the inner child that has been seeking your love and attention.
How to spot the inner child? Well, have you ever shouted at someone, or had a tantrum over nothing and the person opposite you just looks at you in astonishment, wondering what just happened? That, as a whole, is your inner child seeking its needs.

I know when I am low on energy, feeling hungry, little Stephie seeks my attention. She becomes irritable, snappy, seeking her needs. Can you relate to this? Having self-awareness and tending to your inner child's needs will help you manage that aspect of yourself. It is an aspect constructed within the mind, the Lower Self (unconscious mind). This term comes from The Three Selves of Ho'omana, one of the Hawaiians' Ancient Teachings. I will use this model to explain the three selves; it is all constructed within your mind/psyche.

The Ancient teaching tells us we are made of three minds, and the goal is to integrate all three. The Conscious mind connects to the Unconscious mind, and the Unconscious mind connects to the Higher Consciousness. Each of the minds connects to one another by the fourth element, the life force energy. Interestingly, the

Hawaiians call the life force energy 'Mana,' and the word 'Ho'omana' means to empower, meaning that you are empowered when having life force energy. Really ponder this. One of the teaching purposes was to increase one's life force energy and unleash their power and thus their ability to co-create their lives.

These are the three aspects of the mind:

Unihipili (the Lower Self), Unconscious Self, below consciousness - emotions, memory, trauma. Located at the Solar Plexus.

Uhane (the Middle self), Conscious Self - reasonable and rational. Located in the head.

Aumakua (the Higher Self) - Higher Conscious Mind - Higher Consciousness. Located about 1.5 M above the head.

All aspects must integrate within your psyche to unlock your full potential as an empowered, conscious individual to create a life of abundance. Full integration is bringing the unintegrated aspects of the psyche to awareness (light).

The inner child shows up when you least expect it, mostly when you are tired, hungry, and fearful—in your survival state. The false ego persona creeps in when you find yourself in those states, and that is when you are more susceptible to the stories you tell yourself, stemming from the limiting beliefs. It is when you are in fight-or-flight mode, the sympathetic nervous system, and in that mode, your body prepares you to fight or flight, it thinks to run away from danger; back with our ancestors, it would have been a 'tiger.' We do not have tigers chasing us in modern society, but we do have stress and anxiety. Many people spend most of their time in the sympathetic nervous system, the flight or fight. It is not a bad thing, but far too much time is spent in that mode, and there has to be a balance between the Sympathetic and Parasympathetic Nervous systems. So the point here is when you are in fight or flight, the survival state, your inner child pops up, seeking its needs. Think of it as a little girl or boy wanting their bedtime, playtime, or to express themselves.

The little girl or boy needs you.

I covered earlier in the book the need to meet your needs, and whatever unmet needs you have, you will seek partners, friends, family, colleagues, or situations to meet them. Having awareness and responding consciously will put you in the driver's seat. The moment you hold yourself accountable for your actions and behaviors is the moment that you step into the Middle self, conscious mind (reason, rational). When acting from your feelings and impulses, it is the moment that the child wants your attention. Your job is to be aware of this and responsibly tend to the inner child.

I call my inner child 'little Stephie.' I have a few pictures out on my shelf of me as a child and greet her every morning. She loves drawing, painting, doing anything creative, ice cream, chocolate, peanut butter and toasts, she loves her food, so those are a few things she likes. She loves playing with her puppy. She has wanted a dog for ages, and for years I had ignored her request, and I finally listened. I had to listen and pay attention to her needs. For many years I had ignored her, as I had never heard of the term 'inner child', and when I did, I continued to ignore her. I procrastinated because I did not know what to do, and when I had the information, I still procrastinated because I felt it to be unimportant, and I had other priorities, but then came a time when I just had to listen to her.

Believe me, your inner child is your priority. Think of all the times when you acted out and had a tantrum in your adult life. Afterwards, did you feel embarrassment or regret after calming yourself down? That is when the Middle/Conscious self presents reason, and the embarrassment and regret kicks in.

When your inner child screams out for your attention, and you are already at the point of no return, feel the emotions, let them pass through and let them go; see them like the weather. Just as in the UK, you can have all four seasons playing out in a single day—one minute it can rain, followed by sunshine, then next, there could be snow—you just have to let your emotions pass through. The more you practice and start being comfortable allowing your emotions to pass, the easier your life will be. Do not disrupt your emotions. Feel them fully, let them pass through and let them go. It can take a couple of minutes, no longer when uninterrupted, for them to pass through. The deep-rooted emotions can take longer. Just keep tuning in and feel when your emotions have passed through.

Your mother and father did the best they could with the information they had, and the areas that need addressing are now your responsibility for reconciliation, to recognize your wholeness. Your parents or caregivers are not to blame for your traumas. They, too, were projected onto them from their parents or caregivers; and it goes back to our ancestors (ancestral wounds). By blaming your parents or caregivers, you are giving your power away; thus, you will not heal or reconcile with your wounds. Remember, taking 100% responsibility; being accountable gives you back your power; taking back control. When you blame others, the ball is in their court, and you cannot do much, and you become a victim of life's circumstances. You want to take back that control, get the ball back in your court, take back your 'crown', and do the inner work. Now that's empowerment.
Be the creator of your life. No one else is responsible for it.

Your inner child needs you. Now be a loving parent.

Get a second journal dedicated to your inner child and go through the exercise step by step.

Step 1 - Get your Inner Child Journal.

Step 2 - Get a Picture of yourself when you were a child - use your intuition in choosing your picture.

Step 3 - Stick the picture in your journal, start drawing or painting intuitively; use coloring pens, watercolors, colored pencils, or whatever medium you feel called to. Get creative and imagine yourself as a child drawing or painting in the journal. Let go of all rigidity or judgments, and flow with your paintbrush or coloring pencil. The outcome does not matter to anyone but you. There is no need for it to be a perfect and beautiful journal. It has to express you; your expression matters most.

Step 4 - Go to a quiet place where you will not be disturbed. Quiet the mind by taking 10 Deep Diaphragmatic Breaths, inhaling and exhaling through the nose only (triggers neuroreceptors to signal safety).

Step 5 - Close your eyes and ask your inner child what he or she needs. You can wait until they are finished and then write in your journal or write in your journal whilst feeling or hearing their needs. What does she or he need in life? Is it play, recognition, validation, love, acceptance, fun? Do not judge this process; just go with it. This may get emotional; feel your emotions fully, let them pass and release, do not interrupt them.

Step 6 - Ask your inner child for anything else they need and write it down.

Step 7 - Analyze all answers and see what needs addressing.

Step 8 - Make an action plan and block times throughout the week when you can meet your inner child's needs or anything else he or she has requested.

Please do not skip this exercise; nurture your inner child, understand her or his needs, and in return, this will enable you to be more in control of yourself and your life.

Now when your inner child surfaces—and that is ok, it will happen—meet their needs. For example, an event triggers you; your boss does not validate your idea. You may take it personally or feel hurt. You may get into your head, maybe you end up thinking you are not good enough, and the stories go on. Ultimately, he or she seeks validation. At that moment, reassure and validate the inner child. See yourself reassuring and talking to the inner child; visualize this, acknowledging him or her. Make him or her see the truth instead of the misunderstanding. What is the truth? The more you nurture and re-parent your inner child, the more you will find your dynamics with other people change as you tend to your inner child. This will take practice; stay with it, be patient. Stay committed and consistent with this process; you will notice a difference in yourself. Write your observations in your journal; this will help you see the progress and encourage you to nourish that aspect of yourself.

All children want to express themselves, so let her or him do so. Block out a time for your child to be nurtured; this is about waking up the innocence and playfulness within you that we all once buried. Wake up to the beautiful, innocent, playful child you once were.

All this work is going to require patience, compassion, and kindness. That aspect of your psyche is a child; so speak to it to as a child, be gentle. The aim is to remember who you are by letting go of all you are not.

FRAGMENTATION CLEARING

This topic is not favorable for most; it is quite uncomfortable; we do not wish to acknowledge or speak about it. I understand I did not for a long time. Projecting onto people and blaming the outer world seemed much easier. However, that placed me in a state of powerlessness.

This topic will take a deep level of self-honesty in order to take back your power. You are going to have to retrieve fragmented soul aspects of yourself. Reclaiming your power is about reclaiming yourself (the whole of you) and ultimately reclaiming your energy to create a life you dream of.
If you get triggered, take it as a good sign. Triggers are remarkable teachers, so I encourage you to get curious instead of defending the false ego persona.

Some of you may know of this topic as shadow work; ultimately, it is fragmentation clearing and learning to discern the false ego persona (distorted/reversed consciousness) and the higher self (coherent consciousness). A reversed/fragmented consciousness consumes you, and a coherent consciousness will energize and vitalize you. Notice when you connect to the distorted (energy that consumes) or coherent (energy that vitalizes) consciousness. The coherent consciousness is always present, but our limitations are the limitations that connect us to the distorted consciousness. We have access to both, and it is up to us to connect to every given moment. Think of the distorted consciousness that spirals down and consumes you and the coherent consciousness that spirals to uplift and vitalize you.

Fragmentation clearing is clearing a distorted consciousness within the self. Fragmentation clearing is like diving into a distorted realm; it can sometimes feel you are in a 'living nightmare,' desperate to wake up to a 'better, feel-good reality.' The shadow self is forgotten parts of you that have been suppressed, rejected, denied, shamed, or separated from the higher self—cast out of the psyche. To reclaim oneself, one must dive deep into this realm to reclaim the fragmented soul aspects of self.

This process is about illuminating your shadow (your traumas/ wounds) and clearing the fragmented soul aspects; it is like going into a dark cupboard and lighting it with a candle, seeing the actual reality with equanimity rather than your filters or distorted perceptions. When I speak of illuminating, I mean 'awareness,' placing awareness onto the shadow, which will no longer control you.

I honor you for being here; I acknowledge you, and I am with you. I know it takes great courage to face oneself.

Clearing the fragmented self is like when you are spiraling down, with negative self-talk, rage, jealousy, self-pity or anything really that drives you primarily in your head. You see everything distorted, and yet you believe it to be true for you. It feels like a descending timeline, and once you finally wake up to the truth, you are back to reality if you like and feel a sense of relief.

When triggered, this has happened to me, spiraling into a descending timeline, out of control with negative self-talk, and pointing fingers at the external. Yet in that descending timeline is an opportunity to acknowledge, feel, and release the pain.

If the pain could speak...

Once you have that awareness and see the actual reality, a scenario could be 'I felt rejected by another; however, I am aware of the misunderstanding; that is nothing to do with them, but an aspect of the self.' That awareness alone illuminates that rejected aspect of self, and that recognition can allow the pain and emotions to pass through without judgment of self and others. The aim is to know who you truly are; self-knowledge is your goal. That is your purpose, really, to recognize your wholeness. Life shows who you are not through the self-image, the false ego persona, and it is up to you to choose a life based on the Lower self or the Higher self. Neutralize the holds on you. What have you suppressed, denied, or rejected about yourself? When did this first happen? Was it when Mum, Dad, a caregiver or a teacher shamed you with their perception?

What we do not heal, we project onto others; it is time to reclaim the 'whole self.' Do not dwell on the shadow or embody it, but simply be aware of it with equanimity and transcend the distorted consciousness (dark) into 'awareness' (light). This is all about transcendence and alchemy. Turn the shadow into gold for you. Transcend and alchemize everything, all that you feel and hear. Take nothing personally, but get curious about what life is showing you. Transcend the shadows into gifts, and embody new levels of awareness, and every time you do so, life will open up another level for you.

When growing up, I remember Dad shaming me for my sexual preference. I was in my bedroom, in my safe space, and heard Dad furiously heading toward my door, banging on it with his crutch. I froze and panicked about whether he would come into my room. Mum stood right in front of it, shielding me from him. He seemed angry and argued with Mum for a while, and in the heat of the moment, he shouted, 'Your daughter is a dyke.' Those five words penetrated my whole being; my entire body trembled. I stood still, and from that moment, shame came to stay. In my heart, I know he didn't mean any harm by it. He was very open-minded, but that careless comment in the heat of a moment caused years of an injury. I was so young and susceptible to his comment, and immediately I felt ashamed of my sexual identity. I felt ashamed of who I was becoming, so I hid my sexual preferences/identity from Mum (even though she knew) and my family, whom I thought would not understand. I interpreted it as something shameful. I did not fully accept myself, and there was a cut-off, a disconnection to my higher self as I identified with the shame. Holding on to the shame of being gay, rejecting that aspect of myself, led me to project on to the external world. I projected onto other gay women who had accepted their sexual identity entirely and felt comfortable in their skin. Deep down, I wanted to own that, 'being comfortable and fully accepting myself,' but without self-awareness, I fell short and projected onto them.

When I began the fragmentation clearing, I realized that those were my projections. I recognized that my ego persona carried the shame of its sexual identity, and the moment I became aware and understood, I felt something in my heart. I cannot fully explain, but it was like something had taken hold of my heart, a type of relief, or being at peace. Having that understanding with compassion and without judgment did something to me. I no longer felt conflicted inside myself. It felt like I had finally arrived.

By doing the fragmentation clearing, I see my wholeness with more compassion, and I have regained control of my life with self-awareness. However, this work is ongoing, and I still, to this day, do the fragmentation clearing. It is liberating when you hold yourself accountable when projecting onto others; it is not, I would say, delightful and can torment one's psyche (do not let this put you off). However, coming out on the other side is an inexplicable feeling—a grand, miraculous feeling.

When you get out of your head and let go of the drama, you open up to embodying the gift. Once you embody 'the gift' to every shadow aspect of the self, you expand your consciousness (once you expand, you cannot go back to the old self). Keep expanding your consciousness, and you will free up your energy and reclaim yourself.

Do you see how you may have suppressed, denied, shamed, or rejected aspects of yourself?

Step 1. Get your journal, ponder, reflect and write aspects of yourself that you may have suppressed, denied, shamed or rejected, dig deep (block out an hour or two for this exercise).

Step 2. Write brief descriptions of your projections and onto whom, and what you were projecting.

Please note the 'shadows' derive from the distorted consciousness; it does not make who you are. You are ultimately the coherent consciousness, but before aligning yourself fully to it, you need to clear the holds on you and neutralize them by being aware of them and transcending all pain and emotions.

Step 3. Write how often you project onto them. Daily, weekly? (So you know how much time and energy you spend on them; your time is precious.)

Step 4. Write your thoughts, feelings and emotions of your projections. For example, I feel angry, envious, etc.

Do you still wish to carry those emotional charges?

What would you like to experience instead of the projections? (For example, I would like to take a moment to respond calmly before projecting, or I would like to get curious and play with the perceived shadow and see the actual reality.)

Step 5. Go through each projection, and think back: when do you think it first happened; when were you first denied, shamed, or rejected based on that projection (wound/trauma)? For example, Dad 'shamed' me for my 'sexual identity.'

Now think of the present situations. How are you bringing that into your current reality? For example, 'shame of sexual identity;' projecting onto other gay women.

Step 6. Write how you could reconcile the past and present situations, and the actual reality of those projections. For example, knowing that projection has nothing to do with them, but the shame of my sexual identity, I will become self-aware when triggered. I will affirm that I accept and love myself fully. Something along those lines that brings you peace within yourself; it has to be personal.

Please do this work step by step, which will help you reclaim your power, yourself, and your life.
Keep repeating this clearing process, daily, weekly, as much as you like, until they no longer bother you. When you get triggered,

please have patience and compassion for yourself and others. They are all misunderstandings. This is an ongoing process, and they will keep coming until you have an awareness of your projections. Ninety percent of the healing is awareness, and it reconciles the part of you that was once forgotten.

There are also 'Light' projections; what you admire in others is what you have within you—'positive' traits/attributes if you like—that you wish to bring forth in life, such as if you project onto someone as generous and beautiful, those are the traits within you which you will see in others. The 'Light' projections are the self's potential, wishing to express itself and come forth in life. When you recognize those attributes, own them and bring them into your reality. For example, I would project onto my coaches how authentic and conscious they are. Those attributes are within the self, and I see them in the external world through my coaches. I finally owned them and brought them forth into my reality. I say finally, as there was an aspect of myself echoing in the background whispering, 'Oh, so you think you are authentic and conscious.' If similar discouraging self-talk comes up, thank the feedback for its concern and move on. You came here to be a powerful co-creator, so own them.

For those who have done the exercise, I congratulate and honor you. The first step is always challenging; however, once you pluck up the courage and take action, the process becomes much more comfortable. Please move on to the next section.

Know that it is ok for those who are stuck, but note that by choosing to stay where you are, you will keep on recycling similar experiences, and empowerment is about doing the inner work and choosing to live life consciously. I understand if you procrastinate; I have been there. It took me forever to take the first step in re-parenting my inner child. I knew I had to do it, but the familiar and the fear of the unknown kept pulling me back. By not taking action, I suffered the consequences by recycling similar experiences, leading to more frustration and exhaustion.

The familiar is where you feel safe and comfortable, but realize familiar does not mean that it is for your highest good. For example, my fearful, chaotic environment in my younger years became familiar; the trauma-bonded relationships became familiar, but they were not for my highest good. Choosing other than the familiarity of your traumas expands your perspective in life. It is all about perception; perception holds the key to your freedom.

By doing the inner work, you will free yourself from the false ego persona. Right now, you are defending, justifying the self-image which is not you; it is an accumulation of personal, ancestral and collective wounds, none of which belong to you. Who are you outside of those?

The more you hold on to those wounds, the more you are enslaved to them. They dictate your life, and you may not think so, but you will feel liberated once you are truly honest with yourself.
Take your journal and write any resistance. What thoughts are going through your mind? Name what is holding you back from looking in the fragmented aspects of self, the forgotten aspects that have been shamed, denied, rejected or suppressed. It is time to bring them into awareness. With practice, the triggers will no longer hold you hostage, only awareness and understanding of the self.
By practicing awareness and reconciliation of the wounds, you will take a step back and see the trigger for what it is and respond differently rather than react to the same old patterns. Responding to triggers with awareness, time and time again, they will no longer have a hold on you. It will take repetition to unlearn all from the ego persona. So take your time, be patient, be gentle, be kind, be understanding, and be compassionate with yourself because you matter. The world needs you because you are that frequency of love, so be precisely that.

STAGE 3

RECLAIM YOUR POWER

RECLAIMING YOUR OWN AUTHORITY

I once had a supervisor, and it became clear after a while, it was a reminder of whether I had really learned my lesson. It is funny how people and situations come to you either to show you what needs addressing or test you if you have learned your lesson. Have you ever felt that? You learn something new or heal something, and it tests you afterwards? Or perhaps it is the residues of the wounds reflecting back to us. Either way, it served its purpose and led me to where I needed to be. I was codependent on people perceived as authorities; they were not really an authority but had gained a 'status.'

The notion that authorities have power over people due to their 'status' is rather a distorted view. We are all our own authorities and reclaiming that is vital to reclaiming your power. The supervisor I had had gained a 'status' and perceived themselves as an authority. I began noticing myself giving my power away to the supervisor by people-pleasing. I came to recognize this, contemplated, and took action in doing the inner work.

Boundaries were crossed, so I began placing healthy boundaries to preserve my energy. I felt my third chakra/solar plexus, my personal power, was really getting a test. I could feel my inner child (Lower self) wanting to be a good girl, validated, whilst the parent (Middle self) was pulling the inner child back to centre with reassurance. It felt like a wave, a dance between the inner child (Lower self) and the conscious parent (Middle self). I could see the inner child wanting to be seen, and there were times I gave my power away to the thoughts of 'I am not doing enough, I need to work harder,' which was also the perfectionist in me wanting to be perfect.

I had developed perfectionism over the years as a coping mechanism to not get criticized by Dad, and to this day, it plays out in my current reality; I really have to be self-aware and not let it consume me. Perfectionism makes me strive for excellence, and I love that, but the downfall is that I can end up overworking when the limiting belief 'I am not good enough' has its way, something I regularly watch for.

The world pandemic began February 2020. The cobra meeting came out, and fear and panic were roaming around. Working remotely from home was not foreign to me, and I really thought it would have blown over by now, and yet here we are still in lockdown. As you all know, being in this situation is rather challenging, and reclaiming my authority was being tested, time and time again.
I could feel life pushing me to lead myself. Still, the inner child was afraid of being its own authority. The Middle self and the Higher self knew Little Stephie needed reassurance, and both aspects had to step in. Those months were a test. I really had to step into my power with strength, humility and compassion, not giving in to fear and the panic across the world. This was an opportunity to lead myself; no one else was going to do it for me. This was unknown territory, and who knows the best way to respond and act. I had to reclaim my power and not let the pandemic consume me. I really had to listen to my inner guidance, the spaces, the pauses in life and see where to respond in life.

My priority became very clear to me: Self-care.

I really had to notch up on my self-care routine. Even though I have a morning ritual, I still felt it was not enough. I upped my game and added 20 to 30 minutes of reading a day (to address my mental health) on top of the personal development courses, and whenever I could, I would take in some sunshine (vitamin D), and that would really boost my energy. Staying in contact with friends and family, getting enough sleep and rest was also needed. Self-care is essential.

Whenever you take care of your physical and mental well-being, you are saying to yourself that you honor and respect the self; you say, 'I matter,' and with that self-respect comes your higher power. Your aim is to be in your higher power, and by that, you reclaim your own authority. You become less susceptible to your external environment, helping you stand in your power. Self-care activities replenish your life force energy; aim for your vessel (body) to consist more of your life force energy. This will help you reclaim your Power, your Life, 'Yourself.' I cannot stress enough how important it is to replenish your life force energy. When you master this, no one or nothing can sway you off your center, 'Standing in Your Power.'

By aligning with your god-self, you are reclaiming your own authority. Every time you give your power away to external situations, relationships, work—anything that makes you think you are less than your god-self—you are giving them permission to be your authority. Society, culture, teachers, parents, caregivers have taught us to submit our power and consent to authorities. We are all part of this structure; however, you can still reclaim your own authority. No one has power over you unless you give them your consent. I still get caught up in life, but my attitude has changed to focus back to center as swiftly as possible. When you get caught up, focus on yourself, no matter how long it takes, get back to centre, and do not forget who you are and how powerful you can be.

Mum had always shown us to get up every time life tried to beat us down. We had a Lioness roaring for us all in the family. Her inner strength came from a lineage of powerful women. My sister and I watched Mum being a resilient woman whilst growing up; my mum is tinier than me (about 4' 11") but has a heart of a Lion. That is where we got it from, my sister and I. We modeled her inner strength and resilience, and she has always stood her ground.

On a very bizarre afternoon when I was around 14 years old, on my way home, and out of nowhere, a few girls turned up harassing me.

My skin color somewhat displeased them. It was absurd, so I ran as they threatened me with their limited perspective. They chased me all the way home with racial abuse and threats. I banged on my front door as they approached me with a thirst for a physical threat this time. My mum, being 4' 11", stood her ground as a Powerful Lioness, and the girls never bothered me again.

All those years growing up, I modeled my mum's inner strength. When adversity came knocking on my door, I would pick myself up and carry on. This is where I got it all from, the lineage of those Powerful Women. They were Mothers and Wives and had children passing on their 'Heart of a Lion'.

My inner strength came from the feminine energy, the Essence; however, I later realized that the Essence (Feminine energy) also needed Consciousness (Masculine energy) in order to be Authentically Powerful. As mentioned earlier, the feminine and masculine energies have nothing to do with what the mind has identified with. Both genders have both cosmic energies stemming from the Divine Consciousness; needing each other, the aim for us all is to balance both and transcend them into One consciousness. Look at the Feminine as an Essence, a Sound field and the Masculine as Consciousness and Thought Form—cosmic energies rather than male or female energies. Both energies need to transcend as one, so we are no longer identified as feminine or masculine, but One Cosmic Energy.

Going back to the pandemic, the first few months for me were uncertain, and my anxieties were on the rise. A simple task like going to the shop seemed never-ending: the mask, the hand sanitizer, the endless washing of the hands and disinfecting food packages and the space upon arriving, the bags, the clothes were all overwhelming. There were times I felt overwhelmed and tired, and other times I was happy and grateful to be at home. It was a mixture of emotions, but overall I was content.

As you do the inner work and start prioritizing yourself, you will learn to appreciate self-care, you will realize how important you are, and you might wish to align with your higher self more often. The ego persona creates busyness and distractions to keep you from doing it, but if you are really serious about taking back your power, prioritize yourself. Refuel your energy; your life force energy, as I mentioned earlier. A low energy/vibration will make you prone to triggers, poor judgment calls, irritability, and the inner child's tantrums.

Reclaim your own authority by being accountable for your state of being and not blaming the world or anyone. Your aim is to be in control of your life, and you do so by taking care of yourself. Replenish your life force energy, so you can easily align with the higher self.

SELF-CARE &
THE HIGHER POWER WEEKLY RITUAL

To make this easier for you, take your existing Higher Power Weekly Ritual and amend it according to your needs and self-care activities.

You will need to carry out five self-care activities every single day as per categories. You should already have two existing activities, so you are only adding three extra activities.

Fill in your Higher Power Weekly Ritual, five self-care activities from Monday to Sunday.

Category A - 1 self-care activity involves moving the body for 30 minutes: walking, Yoga, Pilates, weight training, dancing, etc. (you should already have this from your physical needs).

Category B - 1 self-care activity: mental well-being involves learning something new (reading a book/listening to podcast/ audiobook) at least 20 minutes. (new)

Category C - 1 self-care activity involves connecting to God/ Source/ Divine Consciousness; it could be prayer/meditation/

anything that connects you - that is beyond the ego persona (you should already have this from your spiritual needs).

Category D - 1 self-care activity; involves relationships or friendships: a meaningful message, conversation, connection to your spouse, partner, friend, or family member. Get creative. (new)

Category E - 1 self-care activity; helps you to self-reflect; journaling, contemplating, drawing or writing. (new)

Then at least once a week, have a salt bath to clear your energy.

Remember, all these self-care activities are essential to your well-being, to help you be in your higher power, higher self, higher vibration. Please note being on a low vibration is not a bad thing at all, as long as you do not dwell on those lower frequencies more than needed. Your aim is to ride the waves with ease and grace.

When you experience feelings, emotions, thoughts that may seem unpleasant, honor and accept them; only from a place of acceptance can you move on to whatever you wish. Do not allow them to run your life. Experience them by all means, but stand in your power and reclaim your own authority by letting them pass through. It is not expected that you are on a high vibration 100% of the time, but you are responsible for your choices despite your thoughts, feeling and emotions. Your actions are your responsibility, not what you think and feel. You are accountable for your actions in life, and the self-care ritual will help you navigate your thoughts, feelings and emotions with ease and grace. The more you honor your vessel/your temple, the more self-respect you will have for yourself. The more you keep promises to yourself, the more you will trust yourself, the more trust you have within the self, the more certain you will be, and the more you can rely on yourself.
One reason you keep giving your power away is you do not entirely trust yourself and therefore depend on others. Reclaiming your authority is knowing you can rely on yourself, regardless of uncertainty.

It is all present within you: your power, authority, worthiness. It is all there, but you just have forgotten. We all have been conditioned by culture, society, parents, caregivers, teachers, etc. That is ok, but now is the time to reclaim your power. It all starts with you, and that is the reason behind the self-care activities. They may seem innocent and may seem like a waste of time, but by not honoring yourself, you are already giving your power away to busyness, poor time management, distractions, and the excuses go on. This may trigger some of you, as you may already have a hectic lifestyle, but you will have to prioritize yourself. It all begins with you, and without you, there is no change.

Look at your life and re-evaluate; what is for your highest good and what is not? For example, I used to watch a movie before bedtime and sleep late. Now I no longer do, which naturally happened as I assessed what was for my highest good and what was not. The more I invested my time in things that really mattered to me that would help me evolve forward rather than backwards, the less interested I became in things that did not help me grow. The movie bedtime ritual disappeared and was replaced by my acupressure mat, and the transition was so natural that I remember thinking to myself, *Hang on a minute, I've stopped watching movies in bed—how did I do that?* Well, I did it by investing in myself, prioritizing myself, and that was through my self-care activities. Give it a go. You have nothing to lose. Invest in yourself, and the more you do, the more empowered you will feel.

Now get busy investing in yourself.

Prioritizing yourself is not selfish. I remember Isabel telling me I was too independent at the beginning of the relationship. So I allowed myself to depend on her, to please her, so I would feel love and accepted. The authority I had reclaimed began slipping away. I began giving my power away in the relationship, cutting off my fingers and toes to be with her (disconnected to my higher self), and without them, I needed a crutch to lean on. Isabel became my crutch, and I ended up paying a high price in reclaiming back my authority.

Do not give away your power to a job, a relationship, or any situation to fit in, to feel love, or to make the other person feel more comfortable in your presence. It's not your job to fix anyone. No one needs fixing. Everyone is responsible, accountable for their life choices. If people wish to mistreat you, be honest with yourself and really assess the situation for what it is. It takes courage to see things as they really are and let go of them for your own self-respect. We all want to be happy, and life is far too short, so do not make it fit or justify it to maintain the status quo because, in the long run, you may end up paying a high price. I experienced precisely that by giving my power away. It seemed innocent; it seemed as if I was helping our relationship, but I felt powerless and empty in the end. However, this lesson gave me such wondrous gifts. It led me to my awakening; it led me to a soul connection. I turned all that pain into a beautifully published poetry book. I used that adversity to be the person I am today. I made something out of it and finally turned it into purpose. Your wounds (karma) are the answers to your purpose (dharma); your karma is your dharma and the catalyst to your wisdom.

Our time on Earth is limited, and we were not born to endure suffering or just survive; we were born to thrive in life. We derive from one Source, and that Source is naturally abundant; there is no lack, only limitations created by our minds. When I speak of the gifts, it is a natural phenomenon; it derives from Source, which is abundant, the drama derives from a 'perceived lack'. Most conflicts derive from wanting something from the external because people do not believe they have it within themselves; all they see is lack. Ponder this for a moment. If we all believed our true nature as powerful co-creators, we would need nothing (love, acceptance, validation, etc.), from the external; we would see our inherent wholeness. As abundant beings, we can create anything we wish. Reclaiming your own authority is about being so rooted in your true nature and having that trust within the self to be happy or content at will, to create prosperity at will, to be love at will, and not rely on anything external.

Remember Who You Truly Are.

Power is our birthright. We were born natural, empowered individuals. I say that because when we were babies, we did not give our power away; we did not worry whether we fit in society, whether our hair needed combing, or whether we needed a stylish outfit. It did not matter to us. To me, that is when we were most natural, empowered individuals, then our external environment began conditioning our persona, and that is no fault of anyone. We began building a self-image to fit in, to conform. We were told not to cry, be a good girl or boy, stop being loud, stop fidgeting, and continually told 'who to be' in life. We cannot blame our conditioning, but we can take responsibility.

We all have been conditioned; no longer the true self, the higher self, we became an 'identity' (false ego persona). This conformity robbed our authority, our sovereignty; conformity says the external know better, and we better listen to what they say. You know best. We all know, deep down, what is for our highest good, but the biggest dilemma is whether we have the courage to step out and perhaps be classed as an 'outcast.'

'I AM A SOVEREIGN BEING; I AM SOURCE; I AM FREE.'

When I get caught up in my thoughts, I love to declare aloud five times.

'I AM A SOVEREIGN BEING; I AM SOURCE; I AM FREE.'

This is a declaration I enjoy using to proclaim and recognize myself as Source. Life will always throw challenges, and you may lose yourself momentarily, and that is ok; however, getting caught up longer than needed is unnecessary. The moment you declare yourself as Source is the moment you take back your power from victimhood. Reclaiming your own authority is about having inner freedom within the self and recognizing the Divine within you. All is within you; all is within your reach if you allow it. As mentioned before, Source is naturally abundant energy that evolves and expands, and our nature is to do so. I invite you to use the declaration when you get caught with your thoughts or life. Declare it aloud with conviction five times; really embody the declaration. Recognize your limitless capabilities and reclaim yourself.

Some say we fear our greatest potential.

In secondary school, I entered a rather creative competition. My heart was set on winning the first prize. I remember wishing so hard that my eyes would squint every time I would think about the competition. It became a quest; I would send out intense energy toward winning the first prize, so I was inspired to create Mother Earth. I made her from a piece of white cardboard, colored with blue and green felt tips; she had round eyes, with the biggest smile, and arms that moved from side to side.

On the day of the announcement, Ms. Vera began giving us a speech. I was a few rows away from her. My ears became immune to her voice as I intensely wished again for the first prize. My fists clenched nervously as she was on the verge of announcing the winners. Her mouth moved slower and slower as I focused my energy on winning the prize. As she opened the last envelope, she began hissing the letter 'S' and finally voiced my name. I froze while my mind raced to comprehend what just had happened. I was literally blown away. It felt like I harnessed a high-powered cosmic force to carry out my desire.

In the last year of my degree, my path got a lot clearer and intentional. I worked in a Menswear Department store to support myself financially. The part-time job had helped me to get more creative with my projects. The job was tedious, as I was on my feet for eight hours, but it set me on to the next chapter of my life. I had realized I wanted to work in Menswear Fashion. I was not sure why Menswear, but somehow designing Men's clothing ignited something within me. It made me feel alive.

I was focused and determined to get a job after graduation; the chances were very slim. Only two or three people would graduate out of the year and get their desired career. I had nothing to lose— well, I had already experienced one of my greatest losses, Dad, and that gave me the drive to achieve my desired outcome: to graduate and have a career in the Fashion industry as a Graphic Designer. It was a couple of months after graduation when I was offered a job as a Print Designer. The head of design had spotted my work at the Business Design Centre in Islington, where I had exhibited my printed suits and shirts. The designs were inspired by my visit to Rome. I had merged the Colosseum, the Trevi Fountain, and other sites from my trip. It was a mix of my highly charged emotions and Rome's Essence into my ultimate project, which somehow had worked in my favor.

These are a couple of things that I have manifested (created) in my life. Can you relate to this? Have you ever manifested or created something inexplicable in life? I do not believe it was merely luck, but you probably manifested—created—them. My point here is that we are all co-creators and have the power to create our lives. We just have not been taught to do so; however, it is our responsibility to educate ourselves.

For me, the people who really thrive in life are the dreamers, the ones that really dare to live, the ones that live their purpose, the ones that do not hold back in life, the ones that follow through their persistent inner voice. We all have that inner guidance, and it is different for each of us. We all have a purpose in life. For some, it may be mothers, a single man raising two children, a CEO, a baker, a plumber—it is all different because it is personal for every one of us. For example, my mum's purpose was to bring up two children; that was her dream. There is no need for it to be so extraordinary; it has to be personal, and it has to make you feel alive because that purpose is you, your being; your being-ness is your purpose. Whatever activities bring out that *aliveness/purpose* within you is your calling, and we all have one.

What makes you feel alive?

In our day-to-day life, it is very easy to give up on our dreams in order to survive. We have to provide shelter for ourselves, gather or provide food, pay bills, and so on. We all have been taught to do this, so breaking out from that way of life takes courage; it is a statement that you do not conform like everyone else. When one does not conform, they may become an outcast. A non-conformist in former times would have been thrown out of the community, shamed and cast aside, for daring to be different. Maybe your ancestors experienced that.

Work with your current reality, find ways to not allow yourself to give your power away to your circumstances, reclaim your own authority, do not hold back, dare to dream, and create the life you have always dreamt of.

NERVOUS SYSTEM

I got goosebumps when I first understood the importance of the autonomic nervous system, the sympathetic and parasympathetic, also known as the fight or flight or rest and digest. I first learned the Power of the Breath through my Yoga teacher's training, resulting in further study, a Breath Coaching Training. It was more science-based while still honoring the Eastern teachings of Yoga Breathing. Suddenly everything made sense. For a long time, I misunderstood, feared or avoided the sympathetic nervous system (fight or flight) and thought I should be Zen all day, in the parasympathetic nervous system (rest and digest). The training had taught me it is about striving for balance and being agile as a cat.

C. Wilson Meloncelli states, 'Think of your autonomic nervous system like a volume control. The sympathetic turns the volume up on your organs and glands, while the parasympathetic lowers the volume. Autonomic nervous system (ANS) imbalance is caused by the volume on either side being left on too long.'

Stress is not good or bad unless there's an excessive amount; then an imbalance occurs. Most people are chronically stressed and do not recover particularly well. They manage their recovery from alcohol, nicotine, junk food, or anything to relieve/numb any sort of bad feelings or pain. When we feel bad, we naturally seek to ease the pain, but most people put on a Band-Aid instead of dealing with the root, the cause of the problem (the wound). The autonomic nervous system, if not regulated, will lead you on a destructive path, bad habits to cope with stress, which in the long run is not sustainable or healthy.

It is also important to note when stored trauma comes up, if your autonomic nervous system is not regulated, the sympathetic nervous system activates, and the survival mode takes over. I must emphasize the importance of regulating your autonomic nervous system; please make it one of your priorities in life.

Now let us dive deeper into the two branches. The sympathetic nervous system, the fight or flight, warns you of the dangers you perceive in your world. This was very useful in our primitive days when tigers roamed around. It would unleash chemicals and prepare your body for fight or flight. However, now it is improbable you will find tigers roaming around your streets. The tiger has transformed itself into chronic stress in modern society, placing you in a constant fight-or-flight mode.

The best safe and natural way to manage those two modes is through the breath. Your breathing patterns can impact your mood, heart rate and digestion. The way you breathe throughout your day determines the quality of your well-being.

Deep breathing stimulates the vagus nerve, promoting vagal tone. A high vagal tone means you can respond to your environment well and be agile as a cat. The vagus nerve, the 10th cranial nerve, is the longest of the autonomic nervous system. It controls the heart, lungs and digestive tract. It is technically a pair of nerves but is referred to as a singular nerve, and is mainly responsible for the parasympathetic response. We also know the vagus nerve as the 'trauma nerve'. The aim is to promote a high vagal tone to respond to your environment with ease and grace rather than react to 'perceived threats.'

Overstaying in the sympathetic nervous system will flare up your wounds, lead to burnout, poor health, poor decision making, and I could go on. For a long time, I unconsciously reacted to my environment based on my wounds. A particular wound, as you all know, was the limiting belief 'I am not good enough.' The limiting belief would bring out the perfectionist within me. It would come up and push me to make things perfect or work harder, to the brink of burnout. In the fight-or-flight mode, I found that the wound would run the show. The sympathetic nervous system signaled that I was under threat, producing constant cortisol, and in the end, burning myself out. This is how powerfully a wound can take over if left unchecked. Self-awareness is key.

In later years, when I realized the wound was sneakily sabotaging parts of my life, I finally took back control. I brought in awareness, affirmed supported beliefs and used the diaphragmatic breathing techniques to take me back to the present moment. When you are in a state of autopilot, you are not present. If you drive, you may relate to this: Have you ever driven and found yourself (your thoughts) somewhere else, and when you arrived at your destination, you were not sure how you even got there? This is the state of autopilot. When you have learned something through repetition, your body knows what to do without being fully present, and most people are on autopilot. The dangerous thing about being on autopilot is that it is the subconscious mind running the show. The breathing techniques will bring you back into your body, the present moment, the conscious mind, and that is what you are aiming for: being present and mindful; if not, your subconscious mind takes over.

So concerning your wounds, whenever you feel bad, check in with yourself; why you are feeling bad. Ask yourself if this is a wound being reactivated. If yes, feel the emotions, pause and do the 10 diaphragmatic breaths technique. Your mind will most probably resist, with thoughts such as *I do not have the time, there is too much to do, this is not for me.* Whatever excuse your false ego persona gives you, thank it for its feedback and carry out the breathing technique. This, in time, will become a good habit to adopt, thus creating more control of your life, rather than being run by your wounds.

The nasal cycle

My coaching clients love this technique, the nasal cycle test; it is simple and gives you an idea of your state. You can check whether you are in your fight or flight or rest and digest mode by merely placing your two fingers below your nose, breathing out firmly 3 times, and checking which nostril is dominant. If you feel your breath coming out more from the right nostril, that would mean you are in your sympathetic nervous system. If your breath is coming out more from the left nostril, that would mean you are in your parasympathetic system, rest or digest mode.

The nasal cycle was discovered in 1895 by physician Richard Kayser. It is not an exact science; there is approximately a 10% fail rate; the fail rate concerns people with breathing dysfunctions such as asthma, allergies, or a deviated septum. Expect the nasal cycle to shift every 90-120 minutes, meaning you should expect your nasal cycle to shift from your right nostril (fight or flight) to your left nostril (rest and digest) every 90-120 minutes. The nasal cycle test is a great way to manage your autonomic nervous system, giving you control of your body and your state of being.

Breathing techniques can induce shifts, meaning you can induce the fight-or-flight mode or rest-and-digest mode by the power of your breath. If you find yourself typically in the sympathetic nervous system, you can induce the rest and digest mode using the Balancing Breathing technique.
Start noticing the 90-120-minute nasal cycle. Get into the habit of performing the nasal cycle test three times a day and see which nostril is more dominant (nostril dominance).

Test it when you first wake up in the morning, before or after meals, and before bed.

Write in your Higher Weekly Plan; block out a time when you will perform the nasal cycle test daily.

When doing the tests, if you get thrown off balance or your automatic nervous system is a bit off, note that this is totally normal. You may be possibly be thrown off course by distressing factors such as a work email, a phone call, or anything really that disturbs your state. The key to this is to manage and track your fight or flight and rest and digest modes. The key is to strive for balance, not to be perfect. See this as a dance between the two modes and have fun with it.

Nasal dominance

Left Nostril Dominance
- Right Brain activity/alpha brainwave.
- The parasympathetic nervous system stimulated.
- Feeling calm and creative.
- After a meal.
- Relaxed, sleepy.
- Feeling emotionally connected, empathy and love.
- Feminine.

Right Nostril Dominance
- Left Brain activity/beta brain wave.
- The sympathetic nervous system stimulated.
- Alertness/wakefulness.
- Prepping for physical activity.
- Hunger.
- Anxiety.
- Action.
- Busy work.
- Masculine.

Remember, when performing the nasal cycle test, it is not 100% accurate. Factors can come into play, or perhaps your nasal passageways may be obstructed, but it is often correct.

Before performing any breathing techniques, if you have any health-related issues, please check with your doctor first.

Reclaim Your Power With The Power Of The Breath.

THE POWER OF YOUR BREATH

I feel so fortunate that I live near a park. Living in London can be so overwhelming, especially now during the pandemic.

It was a Sunday afternoon, and Mum joined me on my daily walk. We sat on an abandoned tree trunk laid out in the middle of a park. A familiar torment crept up; a razor-sharp pain cutting through my womanhood, and the discomfort was getting too unbearable. My heart pounded, my breath shortened and I gasped for relief, and yet the pain persisted. I was extremely nervous, I was sweating, and I couldn't see a way out. As I pushed my hands down on the tree trunk trying to find comfort, Mum quietly said, 'Do your breathing technique.' It was the most obvious solution, so why did I not prompt myself to do so in the first place? I was so immersed in the pain that the apparent solution seemed out of reach. I began my breathing technique, one of my favorites—the Box Breathing Technique. After ten rounds, tears poured down my cheeks as I was relieved of my anguish. I finally felt calm, and it was a reassuring feeling. The pain had gone from an extreme 10 to a low 2; it had subsided and I came back to the present moment with immense gratitude and calmness.

As soon as I became certified, I taught Mum a few breathing techniques. Mum has high blood pressure, and the stress of her work was not helping her at all. When the pandemic hit, I was so worried about her. She worked as an 'essential' worker, attending to customers who were frantic and stressed. So I made sure Mum was doing the breathing techniques three times a day: in the morning, before work, after work, and before bed. This was to induce the parasympathetic nervous system, calming the overactive nervous system with the Breath. The Power of the Breath has been so overlooked. It is the most powerful tool you will ever have in your life. A lot of people will look outside for calm, when all the while the solution is right in front of us. Can you relate to this? You seek a solution furiously when all along it has been right in front of you? It happens to me quite often. I have come to realize that I complicate things at times, thinking it should be more complicated than it already is, and yet I find the solution right in front of me and it ends up being so simple. When I overlook simplicity, my logical mind says it has to be harder—well, does it? Do things need to be that complicated?

The breathing techniques may seem too simple to the logical mind, but you can go from stress to calm in less than three minutes. My overactive nervous system went straight back to the parasympathetic mode, signaling my brain I was safe. In the midst of the distress, I was in fight or flight mode, desperately seeking for the pain to stop. My thoughts and feelings buried me in a dead end. It seemed like I had no way out, but Mum reminded me of the simple and effective tool I had taught her.

Most of us have learned that to achieve or overcome an obstacle, it has to be hard or complicated. Don't overlook simplicity. Train your logical mind to look for Simplicity over Complicatedness.

Write in your Higher Weekly Plan; block out a time to perform the Balancing Breathing Technique (the 10 diaphragmatic breaths technique) three times a day. If you wish, you could do it straight after your nasal cycle tests. Note the breathing technique is 'forced mindfulness,' which can also be placed in your Spiritual Needs section.

Here is a script of the Balancing Breathing Technique. This a powerful technique that gives you immediate results (forced mindfulness). Don't underestimate the power of your breath. Use this technique when you feel you need to recenter yourself, get back to the present moment. The more you apply this, the more you will stimulate the vagus nerve, creating a higher vagal tone to respond to your environment with ease and grace.

BALANCE BREATHING TECHNIQUE

Before you begin, please read carefully. If you have any health-related issues, check with your doctor. Breathe only through your nose (triggers neuroreceptors in your nose to signal safety). If you have a blocked nose, breathe through the mouth with pursed lips. It's a 4-count on the inhale and a 4-count on the exhale, and you will do this 10 times for 10 rounds.

You will inhale four counts and exhale four counts; as you inhale, allow the stomach to expand. Use an exaggerated upward movement as if you have a balloon in it, and as you exhale, let your stomach fall.

Use the three yogic phase: As you inhale, use the diaphragm first, then the ribcage, and last the collarbone. To give you more of an idea, it would almost look like this: As you INHALE, your stomach expands first, then your ribcages rises, and then last your collar bone rises. As you EXHALE, your collar bone lowers, then your ribcage, and last your stomach falls. Please visit my website for the audio.

Three yogic phase:
INHALE
Step 1: Diaphragm
Step 2: Intercostal muscles (Ribcage)
Step 3: Accessory muscles (Collar Bone, Neck, Shoulders, Back)

EXHALE
Step 1: Accessory muscles (Collar Bone, Neck, Shoulders, Back)
Step 2: Intercostal muscles (Ribcage)
Step 3: Diaphragm

Now let us begin. To start, take a comfortable seated position on a chair or sit cross-legged on the floor; just make sure you are comfortable, back straight, and stomach is soft and relaxed. If you sit on a chair, make sure you sit at the edge of your seat with your feet planted onto the ground.

Close your eyes, chin parallel to the floor, face and shoulders relaxed.

Inhale 1-2-3-4
Exhale 4-3-2-1

Inhale 1-2-3-4
Exhale 4-3-2-1

Inhale 1-2-3-4
Exhale 4-3-2-1

Inhale 1-2-3-4
Exhale 4-3-2-1

Inhale 1-2-3-4
Exhale 4-3-2-1

Inhale 1-2-3-4
Exhale 4-3-2-1

Inhale 1-2-3-4
Exhale 4-3-2-1

Inhale 1-2-3-4
Exhale 4-3-2-1

Inhale 1-2-3-4
Exhale 4-3-2-1

Inhale 1-2-3-4
Exhale 4-3-2-1

Eyes remain closed. Breathe normally and relax.

WHEN DID YOU FIRST GIVE YOUR POWER AWAY?

I would like you to take the time to reflect on when you first gave your power away. Pause for a moment. Does it correlate with an event or a relationship? For example, with me, it began with Isabel, (she felt I was too independent); I believe it was when I first made an agreement to submit my power to her, creating a disconnection with my higher self. My thought process was, *If I become less independent, this will help our relationship.* This agreement and misunderstanding in my mind led to a descending timeline.

The aim of this exercise is to have awareness. The more you are aware of your limiting beliefs, the less power they have over you.

Write all your answers in your journal. You are going to decipher this to the very last point, so there are no holds over you.

Now let us begin.

Step 1 - Write when you first predominantly gave your power away and why.

Step 2 - Once you have the Why, I encourage you to go deeper. To be accepted, loved? To keep the status quo?

Step 3 - Can you recall how you felt when you did this?

Step 4 - Can you recall other similar memorable events after that? Repeat the previous steps for them.

Step 5 - Now that you have collated all that information, what is the common theme? Write it down.

Step 6 - Ponder and think about your current life right now. What is the common theme popping up in your day-to-day? Write it down.

Step 7 - If emotions come up for you, feel them fully, and release them. Note feeling fully and releasing your emotions heals you. Cry, shout—do anything that releases your emotions until there is nothing left.

This process takes courage, and I really honor you for doing the work.

Congratulations on doing all the steps.

Every time you show up doing the inner work, celebrate yourself. This will encourage you to go further.

It was challenging to face the truths in my life; it seemed easier to suppress them and pretend that they did not exist. It only works for a short time, though, then eventually, your wounds resurface. They raise their heads for your attention. When they do, it feels like your higher self says to you. 'You are now ready to bring them into awareness and release them.' Your body knows what it is capable of. It is a brilliant piece of equipment; it is smart that when it feels you are ready for your traumas to be released, life reflects back those wounds. In different life stages, we have themes where one would feel a particular wound more than another. Trust your higher self; it knows what you can handle.

Any challenges that come our way, life nudges us to address them, saying we are ready. Pay attention to your body and listen to your higher self. Pause in life to receive those messages; slowing down will guide you. Being busy prevents you from listening to your higher self, your inner guidance, so stick to your self-care routines and learn to pause from time to time. In the morning, when I walk my puppy; I practice being present with her; if not, she devours chicken bones from the pavement. She loves jumping onto the ledges and sits there for a while, and in that moment I grab the chance to contemplate.

Can you think of a time in a day when you can contemplate? Sitting on a bus? Waiting in the queue, going for a walk? Consider when you can contemplate and block out a time. Contemplation will help you reach insights, aha moments, allowing you to reconcile wounds, traumas or gain clarity for your next move. Contemplation creates the space leading you to the remembrance of who you are. Contemplation is not overthinking. It is like a wave of energy playing between thoughts and pauses. Those pauses or spaces allow room for insight or an aha moment, leading you to expand your consciousness.

Block out a time when you will contemplate in your Higher Power Weekly Ritual.

THE 1, 2, 3 EXERCISE

The 1, 2, 3 exercise is a tool to release emotions and feelings. You can use it anytime after carrying out this first round.

1. AWARENESS
2. FEEL
3. RELEASE

This exercise is quite simple; we have been so conditioned that it is easy to forget to be an innocent, playful, joyful being. This simple tool will help you align with your true self, your higher self.

The wounds we carry have so much power over us that the paths can lead us to a destructive destination. With AWARENESS, you can reclaim your power, your life, 'yourself.'

AWARENESS (1)
Please write your answers in your journal to the following questions. This is to encourage you to assess your life and amend it if needed.

Why do you do what you do in life? Read this again and slowly let the question sink in, and write whatever comes to mind.

Why do you work where you are?

If you are in a relationship, why do you have that relationship? (Does it provide security or love, etc?)

If you are single, how is your relationship with yourself? How do you treat yourself?

How do you nourish yourself? Is it healthy?

Do you invest in your physical health? If not, why is that?

Do you have any hobbies that make you feel alive or good about yourself? And if not, why not?

Do you prioritize yourself? If not, why not?

Do you think it is selfish to prioritize yourself? Why is that?

Look at your lifestyle. Are you happy with it?

Would you like to change your lifestyle? And if so, can you make a plan and take one baby step toward it today?

Answer these questions honestly. Remember, your ego will try to hide from you, so really dig in; be like a detective and find those cobwebs in your closet.

This exercise aims to bring awareness to why you do what you do in life. Without this crucial awareness, you may allow a life based on other people's views, your conditioning, culture, society, etc. It is up to you to find out. I recognize it takes courage to look inward and admit to oneself that we have been the ones getting in our own way, but pass through the fear, and you will be pleasantly relieved. Reclaim your power and reclaim your life. Bring it all into awareness. You owe it to yourself.

Now that you have brought everything to the surface (awareness), you may have felt emotions; you may have cried or not. Now it is time to let them pass through by feeling *fully* and releasing.

FEEL (2) & RELEASE (3)

To let your emotions and feelings pass through, you merely feel them *fully* and *release them without judgment*; it takes less than two minutes to release them—release until there is nothing left. It sounds simple and yet feeling your emotions *fully* takes a tremendous amount of courage. Most people avoid feeling the pain by numbing themselves or using distractions to not feel the emotions. The pain cries out for our attention, and most people will cast it aside. Behind anger, there is hurt, a wounded inner child, perhaps that was neglected emotionally. Your emotions are the key to your transformation if you know how to navigate them consciously.

Learn to feel *fully* (do not suppress) and release your emotions entirely uninterrupted. Do that consciously. By that, I mean do not take out your frustration on the cashier at the supermarket, for example. If you feel angry or frustrated, perhaps release them privately, but be conscious when releasing them. You may feel under the weather as you release your emotions and feelings, so drink lots of water throughout this process, flushing it out of your system.

I was previously releasing a wound that I thought I had already dealt with, but it showed up. There was brief resistance at first, but I trusted that this was an opportune time to release, so I cried (felt the emotions fully) as much as I could, cursed a bit, understood, accepted and forgave the person. I did not feel great throughout the day, but I honored myself and self-soothed. Self-soothing for me was toast and peanut butter, with a cup of tea. I found comfort within myself, got back to work (working at home), drank lots of water throughout the day, and exercised in the evening (to shift stagnant energies). The day after, I felt pretty damn good about myself and so much lighter. I wanted to explain my process so you know what releasing your emotions and feelings them fully may look like.

Honor your process to recovery. Take it slow when doing this. Be gentle with yourself, and soon enough, you will feel much better. You may feel resistance towards this, and that is quite usual. Take your time, but eventually go through it, and the sooner, the better. Listen to your intuition, and life will present itself when you are ready to feel fully and release.

Trust your path.

After completing this first round, please use it to release _feelings_ and _emotions_ (anger, sadness, fear etc.) _anytime_ — FEEL (2) and RELEASE (3).

FORGIVENESS

This process is critical. Without it, you will carry anger, frustrations, misunderstandings and so on until you reach your deathbed and then realize that, in fact, you have wasted so much time and energy by holding on to things that a person may not recollect.

There are many misunderstandings in life. We really see life through our filters, our perceptions, and as you know by now, our model of reality is based upon our programming. We make assumptions, judgments and act according to our wounds and traumas if unchecked. Forgiveness is for your peace of mind. It is not about condoning behaviors that have hurt you or allowing them back to hurt you again. Forgiveness is about your well-being, so you do not hold on to energies that may hinder your personal growth. Now, let us begin.

Write it all in your journal.

Think of a time where you felt betrayed, rejected or abandoned. Pick one prominent event. Write it down. You can repeat this for other events and people that you need to forgive.

Write out all your emotions, what you felt, and go back to feel and release. If you feel anger, release it. A tip to further release stagnant energies is by moving your body. You can do so with body combat, a run, or punching a punching bag; anything vigorous is excellent for releasing. Keep releasing until you no longer feel the emotions.

Then go to a quiet place where you will not be disturbed. Visualize the person or event that needs forgiving and say aloud, 'I forgive you for...' and fill in the blank with what they/it did. Say it aloud until you are tired of saying it repeatedly, until there is nothing left to give, no more energy, no emotion left.

Visualize a white light bubble around you and a white light bubble around them, from your heart chakra (located slightly to the left at the center of your chest). Visualize a white light cord coming out of it, going away from you into their heart chakra. Once you are connected, send out love to them. Then cut the cord by visualizing a pair of golden scissors cutting the cord between you and them or the event. See them floating away farther away from you until they disappear. Your bit of cord comes back to your heart chakra. Reclaim your white light, and visualize your white light drawing back into your heart chakra, and you seal your heart chakra with your intention (visualize your heart chakra to be whole).

This process neutralizes the energy between you and the person or event. This process is essential, as you do not want to be carrying energies that hold you down; we are all energy. This process is a gift to yourself. I know a few people who cling to and bear grudges, where they have told me that the person who did wrong them does not deserve it, and I could not agree more. However, this is not for them; this is for you and being at peace with yourself.

FORGIVENESS OF THE SELF

This process is for forgiving yourself, the judgments and assumptions that you have made about yourself. There is no point in carrying them. For some of you, it may be hard if you feel that you have done something terribly wrong. Give yourself a break, accept what you did, forgive yourself, and move on to do better. Forgive the version of you that did not know any better. We all do the best with what we have at hand.

Go to a quiet place.
Sit comfortably.
Close your eyes.
Take four diaphragmatic breaths; inhale (four counts), exhale (four counts) only through the nose. If your nose is blocked, then breathe through pursed lips.
Place both hands on your heart chakra. Envision a bright pink light coming from your heart chakra and envision every time you inhale, the pink light gets bigger and bigger. Envision this until you see your entire body surrounded by the pink light bubble—love stemming from you, covering your whole being. Love (frequency, not emotion) really transmutes all.
Bring up the events, traits, things to forgive yourself and visualize them and place both hands on your heart chakra.
Say out loud, 'I forgive myself for... fill in the blank.
Feel what you need to feel fully and release.

Open your eyes and honor yourself for this courageous process. The more you embody acknowledgement, the more you will do the work. Keep it up. I honor you.

Congratulations.

If after completing the forgiving process, thoughts arise from the same theme, declare to yourself again the same previous statement out loud (or repeat the process). Feel what you need and release.

Some stubborn residue may need shaking off as you embody a new version of yourself, outgrowing the older version of you. Throughout your life, you will shed layers that no longer serve you. The aim in life is to evolve and expand as the Divine Consciousness. Constantly contracting and being a limited being goes against our nature, thus creating suffering. There needs to be a balance between contracting and expanding the self.

The false ego persona suffers from perceived limitations (created by the ego), not allowing the higher version of self to be present. All resistances come from the ego, stemming from a fear of the unknown and uncertainty. If you would let your higher self guide you, you will have a much easier time in life, but it is difficult as we have been so conditioned. Regardless, it is our responsibility to recognize our Divinity within the self and be an empowered, conscious individual. All this work is not for the fainthearted. The inner work takes a tremendous amount of willpower and patience. I honor and acknowledge you for clearing the fragmented self; it takes great courage. Free yourself from your self-image, the false ego persona, and reclaim your energy to co-create your life, a life of purpose.

If you were fearless, what would your life look like?

THE NEUTRAL OBSERVER

I covered the steps on reclaiming your own authority through the importance of self-care activities, recognizing your inner power (your higher power), self-reflection/contemplation, journaling, identifying when you first gave your power away, the 1, 2, 3 exercise, forgiving others and forgiving self. Now that you have all those lined up, you want to tie them all together, and you do this by 'Being a Neutral Observer, the Witness.' — stems from Yoga and Vedanta, I invite you to look into the Yoga Sutras.

This process is critical; whilst you are doing the inner work, keep checking in on yourself, checking on the ego persona. All you have been doing so far is a lot of work, and it needs to be monitored. Your self-care activities will keep replenishing your life force energy, helping you stay in your higher power, which will make all this work much more manageable. The process of 'Being the Neutral Observer, the Witness' will come in very handy if you get triggered. Observing from a state of neutrality and responding is your aim.

Being aware of your thoughts before escalating to feelings and emotions will be the best prevention of falling into a downward spiral. If you are in that situation, pause and take 10 diaphragmatic breaths. That alone will put you in the parasympathetic nervous system, calm you down, and signal your brain you are safe.

Take back control when you find yourself caught up in the drama of victimhood. The moment you blame anything in the external world or feel like a victim is when you will need to stop and breathe deeply and slowly. When you find yourself in your head, you most probably will be in a fight-or-flight state, the sympathetic nervous system. The diaphragmatic breathing will help you get back to the rest and digest mode (the parasympathetic nervous system), signaling your brain that you are not being chased by a tiger.

Do not overlook this process. It has helped me a lot when I have found myself stressed out or on the verge of giving my power away to victimhood. The diaphragmatic breathing technique would literally wake me up to the actual reality, and I would be back in the present moment and in control.

Be the observer of your circumstances; do not become them. Think of this as a game: Play with it and do not take it so seriously. This will take the edge off, it will not feel like hard work, and you will be more likely to do this process. The more play you introduce, the easier it is. Give it a go.
The neutral observer merely observes thoughts as if they were clouds or birds in the sky, seeing them from a distance without interacting with them. This will take a lot of practice, but do not get discouraged, as the more you practice, the easier it will become. A reminder for you is to replenish your life force energy, which will help you observe your thoughts with much ease and grace. You will come from your higher power rather than your lower power (ego persona).

Being the Neutral Observer will help you be in control of your life.

Being aware and awake is the Key to Your Transformation; from the ego persona to the Higher self.

When I first began my self-discovery journey, I went to an Ashram in Bangalore, India. I embarked on a Yoga teacher's training lasting 21 days. There were no luxuries there, just a simple place with a vegetable garden. It was exactly what I needed: a humble place where I ate delicious home-cooked food, performed asanas every day and studied the philosophy of Yoga.

In training, I had also purified my body by performing Kriyas, chanting mantras, walking 14 km non-stop by a sacred mountain and meeting saints who had attained enlightenment. Upon my auspicious walk, to my surprise, the saints looked like 'travelers.' That was what my limited mind perceived. As I reflected, I guess they did not concern themselves with cleanliness or shelter. That perplexed me, but I realized they were 'being,' and the external seemed to have no effect on them; they had no desire to allow it to do so. I remember my Yoga Teacher bowing to their feet, which aroused my curiosity. Bowing to one's feet is a mark of submission of ego and facilitates the formation of a subtle transmission of energies.

My point here is that we are so focused on the external world and bound to our desires. The desires are bound to our wounds and traumas. The self-realized saints needed nothing at all from the outer world, no self-care, no materials, no food (or food was provided by the community) in exchange for their presence and in the end, they were appreciated by regular folks who had opened themselves up to a broader perspective. They needed nothing.

The goal of Yoga is 'Moksha'—Liberation, if you like—and when you reach that state, you are no longer bound to your desires. They had reached that ultimate state and no longer needed those things. They were free from desires. Contemplate your desires in life. Remember, I asked you to reflect on 'why you do what you do in life.' This links to your desires related to your wounds.

Write in your journal. Be really honest with yourself. Reflect on your desires. Why do you need such desires?

What are your primary desires in life, and why do you seek them?

Can you perhaps find a link from the desire/s to a wound/s?

Write the link from the desire/s to a wound/s.

Then write as if you have resolved this wound/s. What would become of that desire/s?

Now, how can you reframe the current desire/s in a way that enhances you rather than consumes you?

An example: 'To feel secure, I must achieve financial wealth.' If the desire is unchecked, it can consume you to where you overwork, disregard your health, etc. However, if you are aware of that desire to create security/safety, you can be conscious of your actions and behaviors. With awareness, you can take back control and not allow it to consume you, but use the desire to enhance your lifestyle if you wish. Create security/safety within yourself. All has to come from within. No amount of external force or events will reconcile with the wound.

The aim of this exercise is to assess which desires enhance your well-being and which desires consume you. This is not about eliminating your desires, but if you wish to do so, please go ahead. However, if you have desires you want to keep, make sure they make you feel joyous, expansive, happy, creative rather than desires that make you contract, restrict, limited, or feel small in life. If you wish to self-realize, then your aim would be desire-less, up to where you reach self-realization, and you have none to bound you on this Earth.

HIGHER POWER VS. LOWER POWER

While doing this work (expansion of self), be conscious of the higher or lower power. The higher power comes from your higher self, and the lower power comes from your false ego persona. The lower power is fragile, and unfortunately, it is viewed as a strength when, in reality, it is weak. I speak of vanity, greed, domination, control, manipulation, and I could go on, all fear-based. The higher power does not seek control; it already knows its wholeness. When you are evolving, choose to do the right thing over the easy way out. Be aware of whether you depend on the lower power (ego persona); it can easily be taken away from you by the external world. However, the higher power (higher self) is found internally within the self and cannot be eliminated.

Imagine that you have a person depending on its status, self-image, the false ego persona. It identifies as being the CEO of a company, for example. Take that 'status' out of the equation.
What do you think happens?

I was in a position at a company where the job left me burnt out. I finally took the plunge and walked away from a situation that was depleting my well-being and self-worth. I felt torn for about a year about whether to leave my position. I had worked so hard getting to my 'status;' that is what the false ego persona perceived. It was the job or my well-being. I had allowed the environment to absorb all my energy; the wounds were at play, leading me to destruction. When I left, I felt like a failure. I was lost for a while, and I did not know who I was anymore because I identified with the role that I took on based on the false ego persona.

During the long indecisive dance, I knew deep down something within was telling me to choose myself, my higher self. As I began listening to my higher self and taking action, my higher power gradually emerged, leading me to unimaginable places. Listening and choosing yourself will build a higher power within the self; the action (choosing yourself) is like a muscle that needs repetition. Lead yourself with your higher power and remain humble.

Humility will help you throughout this journey. It will keep the false ego persona in check. As you expand your consciousness, it can either inflate the false ego persona or the higher self. Humility will help you remain grounded. Please do not see humility as being passive. It is about being gracious. Humility is strength and will keep you open to life. The moment you think you know everything and you all have it figured out is the day you will stop growing—no room for expansion. Remember the Divine Consciousness's nature; it is always evolving and expanding.

Allow yourself to be open and try not to let the ego inflate itself. Manage it, but do not feed it; be aware of it, but do not hand over your soul. It is your costume; for now, use it for your highest good and the highest good of all.

Alignment is freedom.

FREEDOM

What does freedom mean to you?

Ponder this for a moment before reading the next sentence. Does freedom mean having a lot of money? A lot of free time? Doing what you love as 'work?' The freedom I speak of is 'inner freedom,' a state to take you to high places, a place where nothing, no one, can affect your state of being. I mentioned earlier 'Moksha,' Liberation, but I would like to give you practical steps to help you have a sense of 'inner freedom,' and I am sure that you will reconnect to the empowered self. Freedom and empowerment go hand in hand. When you no longer give your power away, it is liberating. Standing in your power, remaining in your center, gives you a taste of freedom, a taste of 'Moksha.' If you wish to reach 'Liberation' I suggest following the Yoga path.

Let us get to work; some exercises may repeat from previous ones. Add and adjust according to your personal and individual needs. This is all about making it work for you. Use your inner guidance.

Step 1- Observe your thoughts like a detective. A tip: Set an intention every morning (upon waking) and declare five times, 'I observe my thoughts with ease or effortlessly,' and that will help you be in that state. Try it and observe.

Step 2 - Do not take things personally (the ego takes things personally and seeks to defend itself or be right). People's actions or behaviors are based on their model of reality, their programming, their inner world. It has nothing to do with you. Remember that.

Step 3 - Before helping someone, ask yourself or ask your heart if that is for their highest good. I know some of you may disagree; however, sometimes you disrupt their karma, their learning if you like. By stepping in, you may disrupt their lesson. When you do that, you get entangled in an energetic cobweb. Stay compassionate, kind and empathic, and assess whether to step in.

Step 4 - Move your body. Your emotions are energy in motion/ movement. Every contracting emotion such as anger, frustration, disappointment, and so on can become trapped within your body, so moving your body every day is vital: a walk, a jog, asanas (Yoga) class, a dancing class—anything, really, that moves your body at least 30 minutes a day.

Step 5 - Nourish your body well. Fill your tank with adequate nutrients with plenty of fruits and vegetables; the less meat, the better. Do your research on what would benefit you. You want to aim for alkaline foods and no processed foods if you can, or reduce the amount.

Step 6 - Read or learn something new every day. The nature of the Divine Consciousness is expansion; expand your mind.

Remember, the more you are in your higher power, the more you align with the higher self, and the less the ego persona has a hold on you.

RECLAIMING YOUR WORTHINESS

What does worthiness mean to you?
I want to focus on recognizing your worth. You may have not thought about worthiness before, or perhaps you have, but it is essential to recognize it if you wish to receive the gifts, love and abundance present in life. The moment you realize your worth is the moment you live your authentic life; you realize what is for your highest good or not. Your worth says to people 'I honor and respect myself,' which then emanates as a frequency to the Divine Consciousness; you are worthy of receiving life gifts. If you remain in the drama, you will get more drama because that is all you emanate as a frequency. If you derive from a state of deservingness and worthiness, the easier it is to recognize life's gifts.

Your fragmented self keeps you in the human drama. When you recognize yourself as the higher self, you recognize the gifts, and life becomes priceless. Gifts from the Divine Consciousness are free, such as experiences that bring you wisdom, family, friends, partners, children, walks in the park, time, sunrises and sunsets, and so on. Think about it; those are all priceless. Those moments bring you into a state of feeling whole when you are in full awareness of who you are.

Your entire life is a gift if you acknowledge it and feel worthy of receiving it. Worthiness is knowing we are love, love as a frequency, not an emotion. Aligning with the frequency of love naturally makes us feel whole (we are that frequency). Aligning with our true nature, the higher self recognizes our worthiness, thus recognizing our frequency as a multi-dimensional human being. The wound of unworthiness will keep you in a mental prison. No freedom can be attained if you keep thinking that you are not worthy of life's abundance and gifts. Abundance is always present, but it is our limitations that make us focus on lack.

My puppy is a state of pure love. Seeing her from my side of the table, she does not need to force it. She is just 'being' if you like and embodies the frequency of love.

Recognizing your worthiness is about being present or in full awareness of the present moment, meaning aligning with your higher self. When you are aligned, you naturally emanate a state of love (frequency). Emanating that frequency effortlessly frees you from the bondage that you have created for yourself. The moment you align with your higher self, you cannot help but receive experiences aligned with the frequency of love. If your frequency is mainly of fear, you will attract people, situations, or experiences aligned within that bandwidth.
The more you do the inner work, the more you will raise your consciousness, and the higher the consciousness, the more you will manifest with ease and grace. Your manifestations will come to you much faster, and at that point, you will need to be cautious with your thoughts. The more conscious I became, the more I could manifest quicker. Sometimes a thought or desire could manifest itself instantly or in under 24 hours, depending on the type of desire. So watch your thoughts as you raise your consciousness.

Align with your higher self instead of the ego persona to live a fulfilling life; your higher self knows the path and sees your worthiness already. It does not have any limitations; it is whole; it is you (the higher self) experiencing a human life.

I recall writing a piece of content. I became exhausted, but I was determined to finish a goal that I had set myself. In my tired state, the inner critic presented itself. I was low on energy, I had pushed myself too hard, and the wound of unworthiness popped up. You see, I was low on energy, so my lower power showed up. I stopped as I realized I needed a break from it. That evening, the thoughts from the wound of unworthiness popped up. They presenting themselves, and unconsciously I slipped into numbing my wound by using entertainment. I binge-watched episodes of a series, and the last time I had done that was perhaps a couple of years before that. The ego persona had attached (attachment-lack) itself to the content results rather than the process of creation. I had put pressure on the results because I wanted it to be good enough—nothing wrong with wanting that; however, the energy behind it came from a 'perceived lack.'

The ego persona will always focus on results based on desires derived from our wounds, whereas the higher self focuses on the present, the creative process, and I had allowed myself to get caught up, and the low energy pulled me down even further. It had snuck up on me, and I had not realized it. The ego had justified itself by saying, 'It's ok, don't worry, you don't really binge-watch series, anyway.' I stayed up till 2:00am watching the series. Part of me felt guilty, and the ego kept justifying its action. Binge-watching series is not so much the issue, but the deeper desire, which I did not recognize. I got caught up in it and numbed the wound that needed my attention.

I went back to the content the next day after procrastinating all morning and early afternoon. To my surprise, I was pretty pleased with it. The ego cared more about the desire based on my wound; the higher self cared how engaged I was in the moment. The ego came from a place of unworthiness, distracted me, and numbed the pain of unworthiness in the end. I am telling you all this, so you know how sneaky the ego persona can be.

Do you see/witness your ego? If not, do not worry, but start paying attention and see the excuses and justifications the ego comes up with.

Now let us get to work.

Write in your Journal.

Can you think of a similar situation when you thought you had it under control, but it was really the ego running the show? Write your answers in your journal; be raw and honest with yourself.

Was the event situation due to an unworthy wound? If so, write it down.

Was the event situation due to other wounds? If so, write it down.

If you had not held on to the wound or wounds, how different would have the event or situation been?
Write it down. Be raw and honest with yourself.

With this awareness, what different action will you take when this comes up again, or how would you like to behave concerning the wound or wounds? Write it down.

Keep repeating this process anytime the unworthy wound or other wounds come up.

Now reframe it to a new 'supported belief' or truth.
Write it down.

Write an action to support that new 'supported belief' or truth.

Carry out the action within the day. This will support your new behavior. Always support your 'new supportive beliefs or truth' with aligned actions.

You are an evolving being. Upgrades are necessary, or you will stay stuck and stagnant. Keep doing the work and keep upgrading your operating system.

Now that you have done this process, you will need a reminder of your worthiness or wholeness.
Your reminder is an affirmation that you will use whenever you feel yourself spiraling down to the unworthy wound. So the next time you feel you are heading to a downward spiral, pause and take 10 diaphragmatic breaths. Please do not skip this step; this will trigger the rest and digest mode, the parasympathetic nervous system.

Then repeat five times to yourself, 'I AM WORTHY' and while you do that, bend your knees slightly and feel your energy go onto the ground or the floor (this will ground your energy and neutralize external energies), and as you do this, affirm your mantra.

Despite the technique sounding odd, (I call it the Kung Fu Release Exercise, see page 120) this process draws in your Prana, Chi, or life force energy from the Earth and grounds it. It releases energy that no longer serves you; it releases the old programming from your subconscious mind, which will help the affirmation work more efficiently. Many people teach affirmations, but it just works on the conscious mind, not the subconscious mind. This technique seems innocent, but it is so powerful: It affects the subconscious and conscious mind all at once.

Try this technique and write your experience in your journal: how you felt before and after doing it. Keep a record because this will track your progress, and what you measure improves.

Addressing this wound will carry you forward in life. Commit to this process and give it your all. Be willing to do the inner work. Some days, you may not feel like doing it, and that is when resistance comes into play. Resistance (opposing force) will make you procrastinate, distract you, make excuses, which is ok; however, be aware of it and carry out the inner work. You will continuously be tested, which is more than ok, but show up and persevere.

When you do not feel like doing something, push through your thoughts, feelings, and emotions and do it anyway. As mentioned earlier, that is your ego persona showing up via resistance. It will show up because the old version of you wants you to stay comfortable. The moment you do something unfamiliar, it will do its damnedest to keep you from it and stick to the old ways, and that is normal, but your job is to acknowledge it and move forward despite what you feel. Resistance is an opposing force; you cannot avoid it. Everyone experiences it. The moment you intend to uplevel a new version of yourself or step into the next level of your evolution is when the old version of you will want to drag you down. See it as a program, and stay neutral; do not feed the resistance. The older version of you has served you and taken you to where you are today. It is time to evolve and upgrade your system, as you will find staying stagnant will keep you disconnected from your higher self.

Sometimes life will shake you, and some may grow and evolve, or it shakes you, and some remain in the victim mode and suffer.

Which path will you choose today?

Do the inner work and evolve gracefully.

Above all, the goal is to transcend the need for self-worth from the external and recognize your wholeness.

THE HEART

We have somewhat lost the art of connecting and speaking from the heart. Most left-brainers, who value logic, analytical thinking, language, and numbers, may overlook the heart and may not find much use. The mind needs to be in a state of calm or unity by integrating all aspects of the psyche (the Lower self, the Middle self and the Higher self). Both left and right hemisphere need to balance, in order to reach the union of the masculine and feminine energies. The right hemisphere relates to your intuition, creativity, expression, imagination, and visualization, and the left hemisphere relates to critical thinking, numbers, language, and reasoning. The heart connects to the right hemisphere, whereas the mind connects to the left hemisphere. Both mind and heart need to work as one.

Modern society is mainly based on the left hemisphere. The mind and logic seem to have taken over, and yes, many people use their right hemisphere in terms of creativity and intuition, but there is an imbalance, and the aim is to balance both to reach union. The connection to your heart is your ticket home. Listening to your inner guidance requires a clear connection to your heart. Fears and doubts may cloud your inner wisdom, whispering ideas wrapped in fear. It happened to me often when fear-based thoughts took over and I thought it was my higher self guiding me. Discernment is a must when you do not have that clear connection to your heart.

With practice, you will eventually be able to differentiate between intuition and fear-based thoughts. It can be tricky in the beginning. It took me years to have this inner knowing.

There was a time when I depended on a psychic reader. Before making life-changing decisions, I would go to a psychic for advice. I had not yet developed 100% trust within myself, so I had to seek external help when in truth, all the answers lie within. I had been developing my clairvoyant ability, but the lack of trust within me continued to create doubt. Most of what the psychic would say would be things that I already knew deep down, so they ended being further confirmations. I came to a point where I no longer needed psychic readers, which happened when I was less in my mind and listened to my heart, leading to self-trust and self-belief. Decision making became much easier for me in life. As you do more of the inner work, meditate, and do the self-care activities, you will connect more to your higher self and the Divine Consciousness. A way to connect to the heart is acceptance of others and self, as projections and judgment will keep you in a loop coming from the mind; acceptance comes from the heart.

Accepting yourself and others will neutralize any emotional charges. I still judge, but I choose to not remain in that state. I move on as quickly as, as I have realized that it is based on my programming. I also realized that it did not help my vibration at all, so I would release the judgments by accepting myself and others and reminding myself that is has nothing to do with me. Judgement creates an emotional charge, and you then match the vibration of that charge, so try not to, as it does not help you in your evolution.

Feeling your way through in life is the way to connect to the Divine, to your heart. Have you ever felt your way to a situation? Instead of using your logic, you felt your way to an answer? The feeling is the gateway to your heart.

Do not confuse this with unpleasant feelings like when you stub your little toe or spill coffee on your top. The 'pleasant feelings' I speak of are receptive and calm; those are the feelings I am referring to. The feeling you seek is like when the water is calm, and there are no ripples across the water.

I invite you to do this exercise.

Find a quiet spot.
Close your eyes.
Focus on the breath.
Focus on every inhale and exhale.
As you do, your breathing will slow down. If not, do it until your breathing slows down.
Sit there and pause, and notice how you feel. If you feel agitated, carry out the 10 diaphragmatic breaths technique and notice how you feel. You should feel relaxed.

Once you attain this 'pause,' remember this feeling.

Practice this technique for five minutes once a day. You can add it to your spiritual needs section in your Higher Power Weekly Ritual if you wish. This is the 'pause' you want to achieve when you search your feelings for an answer; by quieting your mind, you can feel your heart communicating with you.

Another way to connect your heart is through exercises. Please consult a doctor before you carry out any exercises if you have any health-related or medical issues. The heart gets pumped, stimulated and also raises your vibration.

Eating green foods also helps to open up the heart chakra. The more open your heart chakra, the more balanced you become, opening up your sensitivity and connecting your inner guidance.

Speaking from your heart awakens it. The more you speak from it, the more you will awaken it.
Practice speaking from the heart by placing your attention on your heart, and as people talk to you, allow them to see your heart. Notice what you feel.

Last of all, being honest with yourself and others clears out energetic cobwebs. Please make sure the truth is relevant, though —no need to blurt out to the cashier in your local supermarket your entire childhood; express honesty, but keep it relevant. The more you accomplish this, the clearer your energetic field and the easier the connection to your heart.

Your heart is the gateway to align with your higher self. Connecting to your heart helps you to go beyond the mind. The aim of all this is to go beyond your conditioning, which is in your mind. It comprises memory and imagination, creating an illusion known as 'Maya' in Hindu philosophy. Your mind is your karma, your desires. You cannot escape from the mind, but you can control it. Become so self-aware that you make it your servant and use it for your highest good and the highest good of all. Do not let it use you.

Your mind is like a maze and can send you on the path to madness if not kept in check. The ego does not rest. It haunts you 24 hours a day, and it is your job to be the warden of your mind and not the prisoner. Do not allow your old programming to dictate your life.

THE RIGHT AND LEFT HEMISPHERE

Both the right and left hemisphere need to be in balance for us to be at our optimal level. This aims to transcend both energies into one, from living a life of duality to a life of Trinity. We are all going back home to source and merging back into one.

All is about transcending back to one, Trinity.

To balance the right and left hemisphere:

USE YOUR NON-DOMINANT HAND as often as you can - when brushing teeth, writing, drawing, drinking your cup of coffee, eating, etc.

ALTERNATE NOSTRIL BREATHING TECHNIQUE (Nadi Shodhana Pranayama) - Science recognizes this practice as stimulating both sides of the brain. Do it 3 times a day before breakfast, lunch and dinner and note the difference within yourself. (Consult a doctor if you have any health-related issues.) I highly recommend you do this breathing technique. Visit my website for instructions.

READING

SOLVING PUZZLES

LEARNING TO PLAY A NEW INSTRUMENT

LEARNING A NEW LANGUAGE

Pick one of these activities and do it once a week. Write it down in your Higher Power Weekly Ritual. You can switch around activities each week. Make it work for you.

THE KUNG FU RELEASE EXERCISE

I have loved Martial Arts ever since I was a little girl. The first Martial Art style I learned was Judo. I remember how painful it was on my knees and shins, but I loved how powerful I felt throwing my opponents onto the mat. I was so little compared to the others, but somehow, the one-arm shoulder throw became my ally and strength in tournaments.

In my teens, I learned Taekwondo and Kick-boxing - for a short time; stretching out my inner thighs excessively put me off. Eventually, I learned external Wing-Chun and then internal Wing-Chun. My Sifu taught us the importance of neutrality. The opponent would not be effective in his or her attack if we directed our energy into the ground, and this process would neutralize my energy. This was great, as a little lady force alone would not help me defend myself. My defense was neutralizing my energy, and that meant they had
no hold on me, no energy to grab onto. So I then applied this principle with myself, neutralizing my energy. External energies could not reach or take hold of me.

As you do the inner work, your aim is to be neutral, not passive, not emotionless, and not weak. Being neutral is like being a 'warrior' who engages in its life force energy only and is not concerned with the external world, consuming its energy. A warrior is persistent in connecting to the coherent consciousness, the cosmic life force energy. It may seem like a battle at first, as every time you connect with the Divine Consciousness (coherent consciousness), the distorted consciousness (reversal/consumes) equally shows up, and it is down to our choices in life: connect to the Divine or Distorted Consciousness (coherent or distorted/reversed).

Whatever energy comes out on a day-to-day basis from people or situations, your job is to neutralize that energy. We live in a trauma-based world; we are bound to trigger each other, which is ok. However, your response matters. Respond and do not react based on your old programming. Your response is your responsibility and becomes your attitude for life.

Now, let us do an exercise to decipher your beliefs using the Kung Fu Release Tool. The less weight in your mind, the more your heart opens.

I invite you to think about where your beliefs come from and if you genuinely agree with them.

Do this exercise for one belief at a time. Repeat this process for other beliefs.

Write in your journal.

Let us decipher your beliefs by first analyzing your thoughts.

Step 1 - Choose a day when you can really play the detective and observe your thoughts throughout the entire day. Write your main thoughts in a little notebook, or record them on a smartphone, however you wish. Once you have your thoughts written, analyze them and see the most prominent pattern. What is it, or what are they? Write it down.

For example, for myself, I used to think repeatedly that 'I didn't do enough,' or 'it's not good enough.' The pattern here is 'not enough.'

Step 2 - Now you have found the prominent pattern. Explore what the limiting belief could be; go to the root. Be like a detective and find it. For me, it seems obvious the limiting belief is 'I am not enough.'

Step 3 - Now you have your limiting belief written. Your job is to flip the script, reframe it so you create a supportive new belief. For example, based on the 'I'm not enough' limiting belief, I reframed it to a supportive new belief, 'I'm more than enough.' (A tip: When you notice your thoughts heading toward your limiting beliefs, try to disrupt them by taking 10 deep diaphragmatic breaths or go for a walk, or change the environment if you can.)

Step 4 - Then bend your knees slightly and feel your energy go into the ground (floor). Affirm your new supportive belief, and say it aloud five times. This will take some practice, so keep affirming your new supportive beliefs.
Keep showing up and practice daily. Remember, the ego is present 24 hours a day. It is not a battle; it is you being aware in a calm and collected manner.

When you find yourself at a neutral point, the mind has been tamed, and your heart opens up. Your aim in life is to be neutral.

Next, I will focus on grounding, helping you neutralize and protect your energy. Everything in the book really is to help you become neutral. Grounding will get you immediate results; however, doing the inner work will get you even more lasting results.

Your attitude to life matters.

GROUNDING

Have you ever heard of grounding?

Grounding is the most potent process that grounds, neutralizes, and protects your energetic body. It will center you and allow you to align with your higher self.

As you are doing the inner work, you must plant both feet on the ground. As you are raising your energy, traumas and wounds may rise and resurface to clear. You will need to keep clearing them, and you will want to be aware of them. Grounding will also make it easier for you to be the observer of your thoughts. Scattered energy (and that will happen if you do not ground your energy) will make you more susceptible to your ego persona. When your energy is all over the place, you are prone to being in your head and losing yourself. Grounding will get you back to center, thus reclaiming your energy.

Grounding relates to the Earth. When you connect to Mother Earth, you align with her frequency, a global electromagnetic resonance (nowadays on the rise). When you ground yourself, you align yourself to that frequency, and you are aligning yourself with her; realigning with the higher self.

The more you realign with who you truly are, the less the ego persona shows up reacting from a wound to wound, defending its self-image time and time again. The less you are in your persona, the more energy you will have for yourself to co-create your life.

Ways to ground yourself:

MEDITATION - Meditating aligns you with the Earth's frequency.

WALKING BAREFOOT ON GRASS (Not cement).

DRINKING LOTS OF WATER - Drinking lots of water flushes out toxins. Your body is comprised of 70% - 85% water.

EATING ROOT VEGETABLES - Potatoes, not fried, Carrots, Beetroots—anything that grows from underground.

ASANAS (Yoga postures) - Especially Sun Salutations.

BREATHWORK - Deep Breathing (Diaphragmatic Breathing)

PRAYER - Connecting to source/god/the Divine helps you reconnect to your higher self, your true self.

CHANTING - Chanting mantras. Chanting 'Om,' for example.

ANY ACTIVITY THAT MAKES YOU PRESENT AND AWARE OF THE MOMENT, AWAY FROM TECHNOLOGY if possible. Technology disconnects you from your higher self if used excessively; use technology as a tool and in moderation. Do not allow it to use you.

CONNECTING WITH PETS - When you authentically connect with pets, they give you joy, a sense of peace. Pets are a bundle of unconditional love.

Reconnect to your innocence.

Choose one activity from the list and implement it into your Higher Power Weekly Ritual, one grounding activity per day.

Do not let the feeling of being overwhelmed get to you. See if you can combine it with a self-care activity or one of your needs.

Here is an example of combining a physical need activity and a grounding activity: a walk in the park or nature for at least 30 minutes. You cover both and save time.

The more grounded you are, the more relaxed/restored you will feel. It will also help you not to take on other people's energy. It allows you to let people be who they are. By grounding yourself, there will be less judgment, criticism or complaints from your side, and you will be less prone to taking on theirs.

THE CRAZY THOUGHT EXERCISE

Have you ever found yourself lost in thoughts?

Many times, I have found myself in the same spot going over something mentally repeatedly, losing 30 minutes or, in the worst-case scenario, hours. A thought can send you on the merry-go-round and drive you to a downward spiral or an upward spiral. An upward spiral will have you come up with inspirational thoughts, thus being a creative force, whereas a downward spiral will have you on the descending timeline and will consume your energy until you drive yourself to destruction.

You must observe your thoughts without judgment. If not, they just lurk in the background, and the more you lower the guard of your auric field, the more they creep in, repeating themselves, and with repetition comes a belief.

As I began my journey as a Coach, a limiting belief (a belief is a repetitive thought) crept in, and that belief pushed me to do more based on fear. The more I thought about it, the more I would apply force. There was a lot of fatigue because my ego was forcing it, and I came not from my higher self. For a few days, my higher self was whispering in the background, 'Address your thoughts,' and I resisted because I believed I was ok. One morning I had enough of feeling lethargic. It was not my 'normal' state, and I did not like it. I finally sat down and addressed my thoughts by using 'The Crazy Thought Exercise.' It freed up a lot of stagnant energy, and I went back to my 'normal' state.

Below is the exercise that addresses your thoughts when you feel you are in a battle with them or trying to control them. Remember, thoughts, feelings and emotions are not who you are. Note that thoughts can come from the collective consciousness, programs, friends, family, strangers or anything really. You are not them, and the best way to handle them is to let them pass through without judgment; however, sometimes a thought may just get stuck in your head, and you may need to clear them out of your energetic field.

Write it all in your journal.

Step 1. First, describe your feelings and emotions; write them down.

Step 2. Now, what is the thought that keeps repeating?

Step 3. What thoughts/stories are you telling yourself? For example, I'm a hopeless husband or wife, I can't do anything right, etc.

Step 4. Do you believe the thoughts/stories to be true? If not, go to step 6. If so, why? If you believe the stories to be true if you stay where you are, what is the 'perceived benefit?' For example, if I am sick, the 'perceived benefit' is I get attention, and people will love me, perhaps. Explore further where it may come from, get to the root; for example, maybe that stems from Mum or Dad, who gave a lot of their attention when you were sick, and that is the only way you know how to receive love and attention.

Step 5. Now think about how you can receive the same benefit but expansively. For example, I can get attention and love by being honest with myself and others, subsequently aligning with my true self. As I do so, I attract authentic love and attention by aligning with my higher self.

Step 6. What is the 'supportive' new story/thought or belief you wish to have?

Step 7. Choose one action that you will carry out within the same day to support your new truth, your 'new way of being.' For example, as I feel safe to be visible, I will have a genuine conversation with someone new.

Celebrate your win; do not forget this bit. The more you introduce positive reinforcements, the more they will stick with you.

A quick way to handle unsupportive thoughts, is to simply say to them. I DO NOT CONSENT, this really works for me, do not look over the simplicity, just give it a go.

Let these habits create supportive behaviors for yourself.

'Habits are the compound interest of self-improvement.' - James Clear, Atomic Habits: An Easy & Proven Way to Build Good Habits & Break Bad Ones

DECIPHER YOUR LIFE PATTERNS

Write in your journal.

Step 1. Choose one pattern or theme (similar relationships or events) that keeps repeating throughout your life. Write it down. Repeat this process with other patterns or themes.

Step 2. Can you think back to a time when it first happened? Write in your journal. For example, attracting similar distorted masculine energies through romantic relationships happened when I first met Isabel.

Step 3. Why do you think this came up? Ask yourself the question, then write in your journal.
If you find this challenging, take 10 diaphragmatic breaths, then write.

Step 4. What is the main limiting belief of the pattern or theme? Write your limiting belief. If you cannot find it right away, keep exploring by journaling more about one specific event and compare to other similar events. Can you see a pattern or theme?

Step 5. Now you have that limiting belief. Go deeper and find out; be honest. What is the benefit of this belief? An example: By keeping myself busy, I remain in the same place in life. It benefits me because becoming my own authority will mean I will have to be responsible for myself and others.

Step 6. Can you go deeper into that 'perceived benefit?' An example: By staying where I am, I stay hidden, and I am safe.

Step 7. Can you reframe the benefit? How could you use that 'perceived benefit' and reframe it more healthily and expansively rather than limited?

Step 8. Add a new behavior/action that supports it. For example, I can provide safety by affirming five times out loud that I'm safe every time I feel uneasy about being visible and strike up a conversation with someone new the same day.

Your limiting beliefs have created a program, a pattern that served the child when growing up, but you are an adult now, and the patterns need to evolve to the next level or disappear altogether. You cannot keep the same programming that you learned as a child; they created themselves to prevent you from feeling the pain again. Any triggers toward that pain activate the limiting beliefs. They come up to protect you from what you encountered as a child, but now it hinders your personal and professional growth. Your beliefs need to evolve and support your growth to unleash your full potential.

The ego persona, self-image, built the programming to survive in this society, but not to go beyond and recognize the divinity within the self. As mentioned before research says we only use 10% of our potential. How about if you began unlocking your full potential?

Consistency and commitment to do the inner work will help you unlock your full potential. You will free up a lot of energy for yourself. What will you do with the freed-up energy? Visualize and feel what it would be like. It is all very possible when you keep putting in the work, so stay committed and consistent.

STAGE 4

YOUR PATH

KNOW YOURSELF

Trusting yourself comes when you truly know yourself.

The Greek sage Socrates advised above all 'Know Thyself,' the ultimate doctrine ever presented in our existence, I believe. How well do you know yourself? The wisdom of knowing who you truly are, will, above all, bring you much inner peace. All the reading and inner work you have been doing reveals all aspects of self (unconscious or conscious). It all goes toward the 'knowing of self.' This entire book is to help you 'know yourself.' Self-knowledge is the ultimate doctrine that beats all self-help books, workshops, retreats, etc. So stay curious, committed and consistent in realizing who you truly are.

Self-knowledge is key to your happiness and life.

YOUR PATH

You have learned the importance of reclaiming your power, your own authority and your worthiness to reclaim who you truly are, a powerful co-creator. The remembrance of the self is an interesting path, and if you stay open to the gifts rather than the drama or the loop of suffering, it will be much easier to embrace whatever life gives you. Stay open in receiving life's gifts, which can present themselves in many shapes or forms such as family, friends, a pet, the sunrises/ sunsets, the tea or coffee you had, the pauses in life. Do not overlook them; remember to slow down. That is when you are authentically aware of life.

As you slow down and really dive into this self-discovery path, you will appreciate the little things in life and open your eyes to the miracles presented every single day. Believe me, this happened to me. It was like life was always present with its gifts, but I was too busy to notice.

If you have been avoiding getting still and doing the inner work, this is your opportunity to do it. If you are doing the inner work, I truly honor you and realize that it takes great courage to show up and commit. You are needed. During this time, all human beings are needed to unravel their full potential and help others in need. Your 'conscious presence' alone helps and creates a ripple effect.

While you are on this path, please honor and respect other people's journeys/processes. With all that you have learned, it may tempt you to give unsolicited advice to your family, friends, or acquaintances who you think need help. It is challenging; however, it's not up to you to determine when they choose this path. Life will invite them to do so. They always know best, their soul knows best, so trust them enough to know better and honor their process.

When I first began the inner work, I wanted to help my loved ones. It is natural; you love them, and you want to help, and you may believe that it will help them, but perhaps their work situation or relationships need to run their course for them to learn the lessons and gifts. We cannot interrupt people's processes; we cannot judge people where they are and compare them to where we are.
I am telling you this because I wanted to help so much, but I learned that their higher self knows best, and it is better to allow people to be unless they ask you for help. Seeing their wholeness will prevent you from judging their process in life. We all awaken at different times, and perhaps the Divine designed it that way; if the Divine can create such intricate snowflakes, imagine what the Divine has intended for us all.

Our lives are not our own; we are part of one consciousness, and the ego persona does not comprehend that. We are all interconnected, woven together into one piece of cloth. All threads count. Our purpose is to discover where we are positioned on that cloth. Your presence is your purpose. Some sages in India would just 'be,' and their presence would impact people's lives by just emanating their light.

As mentioned earlier, purpose does not mean you have to be assigned a massive mission in life. Your purpose is how present and how engaged you are in life.

In remembrance of the self, and by ascending back to source, we will end the most significant wound of all, separation, thus ending the whole drama.

CELEBRATION

Congratulations on reaching this stage. I truly honor you. This journey takes an enormous amount of courage and persistence. Before you ride off into the sunset, please take a moment to acknowledge yourself and all the tremendous work you invested in. Take a moment right now to look back on all your achievements and how far you have come.

Take a deep breath and truly appreciate yourself and this moment. I invite you to celebrate your results, change, transformation or finishing this book. All progress is to be celebrated.

So choose one thing that you will do to celebrate: a spa day, going for a hike, holiday, going for dinner, etc. Make it meaningful to you. This step is essential to do. Remember, every time you acknowledge yourself, you send a positive reinforcement to your being, and the more you practice that, the more you are open to more joyful, expansive experiences.

So congratulations once again. I really hope this book has helped you. If it has, perhaps recommend it to someone who you feel will benefit from it.

All my love,
Stéphanie Escorial

ABOUT THE AUTHOR

Stéphanie is the Founder of Akashabe and created the **Personal Power Life Method**, after her frustrations of feeling powerless. The method uniquely combines Reiki, Kung Fu, Yoga, Shamanism and other modalities and belief systems.

Stéphanie experienced her personal transformation after a distressing heartbreak. Stephanie says, "It was a frantic afternoon when my ex-partner called me to manipulate me yet again. I had enough of the lies, the mental and emotional abuse. This time, it went too far, but I finally stood my ground. It was the beginning of a journey to reclaiming what I repeatedly gave away — my Power."

Stéphanie first became a Reiki Student and Practitioner. She then studied for her Yoga Teacher's Training in an Ashram after experiencing a burnout, leading her to seek answers through her self-discovery path. Stéphanie furthered her knowledge in India through a 500-hour Yoga Teacher's Training, and then studied Shamanism, Personal Coaching, Breath Coaching, and the list goes on.

She is now a Personal Coach, Breath Coach, Certified Yoga Teacher, Reiki Practitioner, Author, Writer and Poet.

Stéphanie's Mission is to *empower people* with simple, effective tools and knowledge to Unleash their Full Potential in their day-to-day life and align with their Empowered Conscious Self—their True Self.

"Most of us have been so conditioned that we fail to see that life is a gift. We focus on meaningless things that bring us false happiness and dissatisfaction. The true meaning of life is seeing the Beauty and the Depth of the Ordinary lives we lead. It is about re-discovering the meaning of life, through our experiences, and not succumbing to powerlessness whenever adversity arises."
Stéphanie Escorial

If you wish to explore Stéphanie's services such as Personal Coaching or Breath Coaching, email stephanie@akashabe.com, or if wish to hear from current and future products, please sign up at www.akashabe.com or www.stephaniescorial.com

NOTES

NOTES

NOTES

Printed in Great Britain
by Amazon

74976125R00088